During the years of Iran's White Revolution...
The remarkable story of a boy who was trained within the King's court.

He was five years old, held power over the food supply, and had free use of the King's Government Stamp. What ensued over the following eight years was a story for the history books, which had been (because of embarrassment to the throne) buried by the Shah of Iran. However, this is the most surprising, heartbreaking and heartwarming true story that one learns about only once in a lifetime. It is my pleasure to make this biography available for readers both young and old. This biography begs the question, "How much good can one young child with a great heart achieve within the world?"

The setting...

The personal life history and relationships between Behrooz Djalili (now Antonio Gellini an American citizen, Founder and Chairman of the World Film Institute) born April 24, 1958 son of Mohammad Reza Djalili, (retired, an former international Ambassador, President of Tehran University (1963-1966) former classmate, friend of and an advisor to the Shah of Iran,—and now in 2017 a renown middle east political scientist/analyst who resides with his wife; Farah (Antonio's mother), in Geneva, Switzerland, and then Head of Economics, Ambassador for Iran and Foreign Minister Abbas Ali Khalatbari, who was a good man, and one of the Shahs high officers whom was unjustly executed, (may he rest in peace) by Ayatollah Khomeini (April 11,1979), and a look into an unknown behind the scenes history of events that happened during the White Revolution in which Dr. Antonio Gellini as a child was personally involved working with those in charge for Iranian reforms at a time when he and his family were working for the king (1963- 1972) and which life story holds the key to understanding some of the unknown influences and first sparks which led to the Iranian Revolution of 1978.

ANTONIO GELLINI
Portrait of a Hollywood Legend

Well Health Books

Ethel C. Richard
Antonio Gellini

All articles, stories, photographs, and information used within this book or in marketing materials relating to this book have been used with permission from Antonio Gellini.

Copyright © 2017 - Ethel C. Richard
United States Historical Society Washington, D.C.
Unusual Political Childhood Biographies of Americans
Part of the *Held in Evidence* Series of Unusual Historic American Biographies

Well Health Publications™
Well Health Books™

Well Health Publications and *Well Health Books* are Trademarks of Ethel C. Richard.

ANTONIO GELLINI

Portrait of a Hollywood Legend

EIGHT YEARS IN IRAN
…a little boy, appointed an Official within the Shah's Government

True life history of Behrooz Djalili
A Commissioned Biography

A Well Health book in cooperation with
Antonio Gellini and The World Film Institute

Ethel C. Richard
Antonio Gellini

SPECIAL NOTE

Recently dignitaries of Greece have honored Dr. Gellini in giving to him a new name, "Olympia Awards Gellini" after the name of the town of origin from where the Olympiad of ancient Greece first sprang in 776 BC and for his important role in bringing back the spirit of Olympia to the arts, and renewed joy to the people of Greece and to the world.

DEDICATION

This book is dedicated to my father Mohammad Reza Djalili and my mom Farah Hojty Vessaly, My very dear late wife Parvin, and to my daughters, Sanaz and Elham. And to the memory and honor of those good people who have passed, and who were important people within my life, including Dr. Abbas Ali Khalatbari, Dick Clark, Jack Valenti, Gene Weed. And to the Work toward World Peace, Diversity of Religion and Culture. To the American People and the American Dream. To former US President Bill Clinton. And also to families and to the world's children who make the world go round! May everyone's future be full of beauty, of cultures, and the arts and of healthy entertainment.

~Dr. Antonio Gellini (Behrooz Djalili)

EIGHT YEARS IN IRAN

The Untold Story of Antonio Gellini

Founder of the World Film Institute, the Family Film Awards, and the all new Olympia Awards—Competitions of Cultures Arts and Entertainment.

A Commissioned Biography

CONTENTS

Acknowledgments
    Ethel C. Richard   13
    Dr. Antonio Gellini   17

Personal Message from Dr. Antonio Gellini   23

Introduction   27

PART ONE - *Life in Iran*

Prologue *"Beginnings"*   33

The Process   49

My Youth   57

Found Out - *The SAVAK Investigation*   69

Coming to America - *Thoughts About the World Film Institute and My Marriage with an Angel Whom I Will Never Forget*   73

Epilogue   75

PART TWO

The Untold Story of Antonio Gellini and the Origins of the World Film Institute   83

A Cozy Iranian Cafe in Westwood   87

Let's Forget the Pomp of Hollywood…   91

The Olympics of the Cultures - *World's Best of Arts and Entertainment*   105

Making History   121

Olympia Awards of Cultures, Arts and Entertainment   133

Message from the Founder   143

ACKNOWLEDGEMENTS
FROM ETHEL C. RICHARD

Of course no biography is complete without having acknowledged the people who help to make it possible to exist.

Firstly, I must sincerely thank Antonio Gellini for having chosen me as the author for his commissioned biography. He has shown tremendous faith in my skills to bring his story to the masses, has spent several months as my friend and has opened up with me in countless conversations in talks and interviews and I with all my heart can only do my very best and then lean on God that my best will meet Antonio's expectations and will also prove to be worthy of accuracy and merit, and as interesting and colorful as the man himself. That we are both spiritually minded people goes without saying and I invite the Living God to bless this effort to bring a "wisely written and sensitive true biography" to fans of this man around the world, and to do justice to his respectability and to his generosity of heart, his great vision and his remarkable life history as well.

The World Film Institute is a California based nonprofit 501 (c)3 corporation, and I as the author of this biography am

ETHEL C. RICHARD
with Dr. Antonio Gellini

doing this work purely as a donating volunteer and will receive no monetary compensation whatsoever from the Institute related to my authorship of or from sales of this book (which is my personal contribution into the furthering of the work of the Institute and toward the education of young and old alike within America and through out the world, and in doing so contributing to International Peace efforts (Mr. Gellini is an honored United Nations International Ambassador for Peace awarded this position through the WCH and Universal Peace Federation in cooperation with UNESCO, and working to promote International Unity through the Arts and Entertainment, in the instituting of Olympia Awards Competitions of Cultures and other international cultural exchange and awards competitions).

All parts of what would be my share from sales as author for this work are donated to the World Film Institute in order to benefit artists and the arts. I am not involved in the production or distributions of this work and so I cannot speak for production costs or for commissions of third parties /book retailers for that is not my affair and is of normal order of business in the publishing field and so is not within my power to dictate.

This is a history book as well as a biography and since my personal friendship with Dr. Gellini also is provable and his life and mine are connected, his biography is technically part of my own biography as well (and my biography already having been accepted into the Historical Societies), still, none the less because his biography stands on its own merit and

ANTONIO GELLINI
Portrait of a Hollywood Legend

involves his past and present personal friendships and family relationships within several international political and entertainment circles, with ambassadors, high level international dignitaries, former presidents of nations and with the royal family of Iran (Mohammad Reza Shah Pahlavi), I am forwarding this biography to William C. DiGiacomantonio, Chief Historian for the United States for inclusion into The United States Historical Society at Washington, DC., where it will be included as an historical biography and therefore suitable and made available for use within children's schools curriculums across America.

Therefore I will also thank Mr. DiGiacomantonio in advance here for his acceptance of this biography as educational material of historical significance for American public grade and middle schools youngsters as part of this endeavor. It will be made available for use within schools libraries both under my name as author of the text and also under Mr. Gellini's Name, listed under and within several historical references related to famous families, Iran, history of the American film industry, United Nations International Humanitarian and Peace Building Programs, and the new Olympias of Cultures, Arts and Entertainment. As I have stated, topics of wide historical interest are included within his biography.

Fair Use excerpts of articles from the *Los Angeles Times* and *People Magazine* have been shared in this book to illustrate pertinent information dealing with film industry practices during the eighties is an essential element in the telling of Dr. Gellini's history—as it was Dr. Gellini's heart

ETHEL C. RICHARD
with Dr. Antonio Gellini

for families, his personal involvement as friends with Jack Valenti (then President of the Motion Picture Association of America), their association and friendship with Dick Clark (Dr. Gellini, founder and President of the World film Institute was in partnership with the famed Dick Clark (Dick Clark Productions), and Dr. Gellini's political activities, his meeting with then President for the United States Bill Clinton—which resulted in being instituted within law important film industry safeguards for production of family films, which brought to accountability the American film industry, destroyed the then existing American film market monopoly, and brought family entertainment into the forefront as a desirable film industry endeavor.

Thank you to former President Bill Clinton for his contribution in helping to make healthy family entertainment more accessible to the American family and thank you to former Vice President Al Gore for his continuing support of the World Film Institute and the Olympia Awards Competitions of Cultures, Arts and Entertainment and of the world wide Family Film Awards

Also, thank you to Justin Wallner (Vice President of the World Film Institute) and to *Javanan Magazine* for their up to date contributions to this biography.

ACKNOWLEDGMENTS
FROM DR. ANTONIO GELLINI

First I give thanks to G-d for my own mom and dad and for our families (Djalili and Vassaly) and then I thank these my parents and our families individually for their love and their support in these endeavors, and special thanks to my publisher, friend and co-author Ethel Richard, and to Keith Katsikas and his wife Rebecca for understanding the value of Cultural Exchange and of the World Film Institute, and Olympia Awards Competitions of Cultures, Arts and Entertainment. My best wishes be to all of you for publishing this historical biography and may it be inspiring other people's from the many nations and especially young people who are believers in dreams of a beautiful future and in continuing this journey of humanitarianism worldwide.

Continuing in this journey: my dear friend and partner President Mr Allan Jay Friedman, Vice President Justin Wallner, my dear friends, Joel Diamond and Rebecca Holden, Kenneth Holm, Koji Mizukami, Alain Zirah and Anne Gomis, Mehdi Zokie, Farhang Farrahi, Mohandas Shajara, Nader Rafiee, Ashkan Tabibnia, Princess Maria Amor, Rossana Huang and Robert Sun.

Thanks to Maryam Morrison, Sonia Été, Nate Nader, Tia

ETHEL C. RICHARD
with Dr. Antonio Gellini

Walker, Dr. Hong Tao-Tze, Pamela Chen, Farah Shokouhi, Fredon Tofeghy, Nader Zemorad. Rocky Jones, Mayor Eric Garcetti, Gil Garcetti, Fonda Dereci, Larry Carpenter, Hassan Khaytbashee, Leslie Bricusse, Soheal Nikbin, Ali Mashkat, Parviz Ghazi Saeed, Jimmy Sedghi, Princess Leith, Lissa Pacheco Chow, Mandy Francisco, Larry Carper and also the Family of Prince Mario Max Schaumburg Lippe (and)

The Family of Byjelvand
The Family of Abrahimi
The Family of Ghabei
The Family of Dardashtee
The Family of Hasimyan

THE WORLD FILM INSTITUTE

On behalf of the Board of Trustees of the World Film Institute we wish to thank the following members of our (original) official family. This "Family Film Awards" telecast, which we were so fortunate to have the opportunity to present, would not have been possible without the commitment and support of the following individuals and organizations.

PRIMESTAR
Denny Wilkinson, Karen Muldoon Geus, Mark Dunn

CBS
Terry Botwick

DICK CLARK PRODUCTIONS

ANTONIO GELLINI
Portrait of a Hollywood Legend

Dick Clark, Gene Weed, Ron Weed, Fran LaMaina

BEVERLY HILLS VIDEO GROUP
Jay Elliot

SFM ENTERTAINMENT
Stan Moger, Jordan Ringel, John Firestone, Lori-Ann Borries, Inyl Holland, John Peebles

MICROSOFT CORPORATION
Bill Gates, Tom McMail, Robyn Pitts, Margaret Smith, Patty Stonesifer

BRISTOL-MYERS SQUIBB
Peggy Kelly, Mary McAllen, Jean D'Agostino,

JOHNSON & JOHNSON
Andrea Alstrup, Jill Lesko, Lisa Cerrato

YOUNG & RUBICAM
Bob Igiel, Tara Campbell

LEO BURNET
Laura Caraccioli (and new baby)

PENTACOM
Marcie Hill

TELVEST
Irwin Gotlieb, Ira Sperling

ADLER BOSCHETTO PEEBLES
Ray Albergotti, Lawrence Boschetto, Tania Sochurek

M. GRANT & ASSOCIATES

ETHEL C. RICHARD
with Dr. Antonio Gellini

Marsha Grant, Stephanie Bloomberg, Carole Evans, Dana Katz, Elyse Klein, Dennis Kain, Dr. Yoshiro NakaMats, Rick Portin, Harold Goldes, Paul Mitchell, Kelly Brock, Ms. Maria Alfonso, Gennaday Levtchenko

THE SHEFRIN COMPANY
Paul Shefrin

NEAL PUBLIC RELATIONS
Roger Neal
Charlton Heston
Richard Thomas
Thomas Ian Nicholas
Joel Diamond

PRINCE OF PRINTS
Randy Quiring

CELLULAR FANTASY
Sia Hodjatie

SCORZA DESIGN AND MARKETING
Salvatore E. Scorza

GOD NEWS TYPESETTING
Daniel L. Hafer, Steven D. Preston

BLUE RIBBON PANEL
Lindsay Wagner

ANTONIO GELLINI
Portrait of a Hollywood Legend

Rose Ganguzza
F.X. Feeney
Joanna Connors
Keith Simanton
Lowell Staine
Henry Deas III
Al Kasha
Shelley Winters
Lynn Smith
Laurin Sydney
Michael Medved
Leonard Klady
Alan Silverman
Laurel Graeber
Duane Byrge
Kenneth Turan
Julie Hirsch
Pat Wise
J. R. Boyd
Neal Rydall
Kari Clark
Neil Sterns
Dick Guttman
Heidi Shaeffer
Brad Cafarelli
Kym Brady
Steve Tellez
Michelle Bega
Karen Smith
Roger Lane
Michelle Adkins
Mark Hahs
Beverly Magid

ETHEL C. RICHARD
with Dr. Antonio Gellini

Ward Grant
Richard Grant
Gayle Khait
Leslie Kitay
James Rowley
Nicole Goesseringer
John Tomich
Sean Bishop
Ronald P. Gardner
Don Camp
Richard Sanches
Camilla Porbe
Michael Simms
Brandon Simms

As Chairman of the World Film Institute's Board of Trustees I want to express my sincere gratitude to our Board of Directors for their unwavering support. A very special thanks to two very special people, Tichi Wilkerson Kassel and Antonio Gellini, for their vision in creating this organization.

- Arthur M. Kassel
Chairman, Board of Directors
(1996) The World Film Institute

PERSONAL MESSAGE FROM DR. ANTONIO GELLINI

My native last name is Djalili (pronounced Jalili) and now as an American citizen my name is Antonio Gellini. I believe that if I am doing something good today, many years after today I have become a very good person, my friends, and my people. We have to know the beauty of the human being, one's care for another. It was a blessing to me in my childhood in Iran the huge diversity of different cultures and different customs which educated me to become an able and decent human being; there are no restrictions, lifestyles or age barriers when it comes to love and I never have found anything more beautiful than when I see someone smiling!

I pass my message to all of my brothers and sisters around the world. This is the light of human beings. It doesn't matter where you are, "I love you, I love you and I love you!"

In the name of creation, G-d bless me in all that I am saying, that it is true and not harming anybody in any way, not my country, or my religion or my mother and father, other family and friends or anybody who knows me from around the world…and of the things that I see which you

ETHEL C. RICHARD
with Dr. Antonio Gellini

do not see, I just want to say something from the bottom of my heart, using my own words and from responsibility, and understanding the beginnings of my heritage.

"Thinking good, acting good, and speaking good". I am not here to focus on which things may be negative within my heritage, but to help people to understand the value of cultures, that it is mainly important that everyone will be proud of themselves, because I believe that we all come from "a little village." In my city where I was born there was a poet and a poem which is known called "Mother" and the poem mentions how your mother brought you into the earth, taught you the alphabet putting it on your lips, how she took your hand, teaching you to walk step by step. My appreciation of mother is in my DNA and is also symbolic of my culture, my heritage.

In my native Iran the way we talk about woman and mother is symbolic of mother earth, and we believe that "air, fire, every stone" show me that this is my home, my house, and mother earth is in front of me, and if I am doing something wrong I have reason to be ashamed. So always, every day, every minute I have chance I look upon beautiful mother earth and it doesn't matter where I am, in whatever country, I say, "I want to be a better person, I want to be a better person. Forgive me mother earth! ...and if I am walking through the sand and I do something wrong of which I am not aware ...please educate me!"

I was born in the holy city which is called the spiritual capital city of Iran, (Mashhad), which has the Tomb of Imam Reza, 8th Shi'i imam in the authority of Iran ...and

ANTONIO GELLINI
Portrait of a Hollywood Legend

the land, the heritage is so good, and many people of good thoughts and good wishes always come into the city to visit into the holy place. I am really respecting my beautiful mom, and my grand mom. They come from the Jewish faith and have an open mind and they really respect the authority of our homeland—and they give even more respect for love and for humanitarianism. That's why we show respect to each other—dogmatically, and I was blessed to learn from my father, to understand how important is mother, and how important are human beings, and so, I always (because of this) focus to behave myself. I respect the women. Also I was born with a gift to accept all people and so though people may be different, perhaps born with a disability and having some problem (for instance, with no hands or blind) I do not see it as a bad thing. I see the person as good and full of potential and I see an opportunity to show love. Mentally, physically, and spiritually, toward any human being… we have to, I believe, love him.

We are part of each other. If my eye hurts then all of my body hurts. If my shoulder hurts then all my body hurts. I perceive for myself for example, that my heart is America, my eye is Iran, and my brain is Israel, and my hands each also hold a different country and this is the point I make …and how I grew up to respect other countries as my own.

INTRODUCTION

Sometimes one comes upon a story that is so remarkable it is near impossible to comprehend... and this is one such story.

When I first got this assignment I thought to myself, "This should be a piece of cake" (very easy because I was certain that this man just wants a simple Hollywood Bio, a promotional book of sorts for the World Film Institute and not too terribly complicated...just the skim the surface superficial kind of material of Hollywood stars). It hasn't turned out the way I'd pictured it however, and what I am left with in my hand after my somewhat intensive investigations is an amazing life story of a remarkable man whom for many years would really have rather that his true most personal story stay hidden from the public forever, so that others will not have even a slight negative word said about them and that only the tremendous beauty of people and cultures and arts of the world will be brought to the front and into the spotlight.

Well I am a writer of realism, history and behind the scenes true news and after he having commissioned me (one of his best friends, and I say this with sincerity because I would always

ETHEL C. RICHARD
with Dr. Antonio Gellini

be fair to this man—as he truly is a sweetheart of a human being), to write his bio, it became evident to me that to do so in any realistic way which will remotely resemble the life history of the real man, (and not merely write a history of the World Film Institute and its offshoots), and to write a Bio which truly does him justice, while being historically factual, that I must place our friendship on the firing line. You see, there is a lot more to Dr. Antonio Gellini than meets the eye and his story is not so satiny smooth nor has it been without blemish, for just as anyone who has had an extremely hard childhood and younger life, his true behind the scenes story has been marked by pain, tragedy of unspeakable proportion and he would really rather leave the past within the past and never speak of things which had happened.

His sensitive and fighting spirit is immeasurably and remarkably strong for him to have continued in his vision for the World Film Institute amidst and in the face of what appear to have been seriously nearly insurmountable odds.

The end result of my work is that this is not the average Hollywood Icon biography. To begin with, Antonio Gellini is NOT the average American man. He is an immigrant Iranian American Citizen (and proud of it) and he is not even the average Iranian, (he having been born in Mashhad, Iran during the Pahlavi reign, the son of an important diplomat and he also having had as a young person some notoriety himself while within Iran, and even just for the fact of whom his family is and of those whom raised him and who were his associates and within the direction which his life took) and so,

ANTONIO GELLINI
Portrait of a Hollywood Legend

he is not the "average" man by anyone's estimation.

Antonio Gellini has the biggest, most giving heart of anyone I have ever known, is working in cooperation with promoted programs accepted under UNESCO, and has received high honors for his work in humanitarian international peace building efforts from two respected United Nations organizations. He is an Ambassador working to further World Peace within Cultural Arts and Entertainment fields and so his affiliation with the United Nations is on an educational and a sociological level, and not on a political level.

Comes to my mind a statement made to me by Dr. Gellini during one of our conversations, "Being a good person. That is my definition of love, to be a good person and to be practical. In childhood we had an old saying, "Scratch my back and I'll scratch yours." Other people accept that lie. I don't expect that somebody will return the favor, and I give. I do good for people. I don't scratch somebody's back hoping to get my back scratched."

Dr. Gellini, a very intelligent man who completed college at 18 years old while still in Iran, and who does speak several languages still struggles some with comprehension and usage of the English language, a fact which many do not fully understand, a result of his having taken English language courses rather late in life. Many times because of this (and because I am partly deaf) he and I have struggled together doing battles within interviews to come down to the elements of his story which are extremely important to the retelling of it through the English language. This book, in the future, will

ETHEL C. RICHARD
with Dr. Antonio Gellini

be made available in several languages throughout the world and so I have made extra effort to be precise so that nothing will be lost in the translations of his biography.

It is my prayer that my efforts will bring you (his fans) closer to an better understanding of who Dr. Antonio Gellini really is and to help you appreciate the inherent goodness of this person whom was once in partnership with, and the close friend of another great American Hollywood Icon and legend, the late Dick Clark (of Dick Clark Productions), who produced the beloved 24 years of "American Bandstand" on ABC Network (from 1957).

Having come to understand Antonio Gellini to the extent that I have I am filled with satisfaction that I have been communing with a remarkable human being and one whom in fact deserves a very tremendous admiration and deepest respect. You will find this book fascinating, for he is a very fascinating human being who has come from an enormously equally fascinating background.

*American Bandstand is an American music-performance show that aired in various versions from 1952 to 1989 and was hosted from 1956 until its final season by Dick Clark, who also served as producer) and the famous Dick Clarks Rockin' New Year's Eve Party. Beginning in 1972 and for four decades Clark would be a welcome guest in American households as host of "Dick Clark's Rockin' New Year's Eve".

PART ONE

Life in Iran

PROLOGUE
Beginnings

"The World Film Institute, Together we're Bridging Cultures, Building Peace around the World and Making a Better, Safer World for our Families... our Men, our Women and our Children"

It is from this setting (Iran) and within the tight knit circles of the Royal Court, the personal friends and Ambassadors of the Shah of Iran from which his story begins...

"In the context of regional turmoil and the Cold War, the Shah established himself as an indispensable ally of the West. Domestically, he advocated reform policies, culminating in the 1963 program known as the White Revolution, which included land reform, the extension of voting rights to women, and the elimination of illiteracy. These measures provoked religious leaders, who feared losing their traditional authority, to raise their voices against him, which consequently led to some civil unrest. And the increasing arbitrariness of the Shah's rule caused more provocation among the intellectuals, who seeking democratic reforms. These opponents criticized the Shah for

ETHEL C. RICHARD
with Dr. Antonio Gellini

subservience to the United States and for violation of the constitution, which placed limits on royal power and provided for a representative government."

-From an article found at:
www.iranchamber.com/history/pahlavi/pahlavi.php

TEHRAN, IRAN (1963)

Antonio explained to me that he'd never had a childhood, at least not in any sense that we in America would consider to be a childhood. It seems to him that he went straight into adulthood, having been removed from his home in Mashhad by his parents and moved into his aunts home at Tehran from a very tender age of approximately 5 years old. He spent eight months living with his aunt and then his care was removed from his aunt, he was moved in again with his parents for a time in Tehran (during the time his father was first appointed Chancellor for Tehran University) and then his years remaining from a young child in Tehran were spent mostly living away from his parents, who were both together and working away from Tehran (many times in foreign countries) and were spent under the care of a nanny (from Russia) and two maids (one from China and the other Taiwan) while he attended school, and while he was working after school doing inventory for his father's close friend, Mr. Abbas Ali Khalatbari who was in charge over the economy for Iran, and whom the young Behrooz Djalili (Antonio Gellini's birth

ANTONIO GELLINI
Portrait of a Hollywood Legend

name) as a child had addressed simply as "uncle."

So right off the bat we know. We have established that Behrooz was not an ordinary child. Behrooz was born into the circle of the Shah's court, he was raised by, mingled with and was trained by very high elite officers who had been appointed, handpicked by the Shah of Iran himself.

Young Behrooz had done so well in his studies of language and writing that he passed his two year assignment within one year while having been in training for government work after morning classes at the grade school and was upon completion of that year placed "on his own" into a very important position of power, working in inventory of foods and agriculture, directing drivers of trucks loaded with foodstuffs for the Iranian government... Behrooz was only still five (yes, even as a five year old boy) when under direction and supervision of the head of economics for Iran, who'd left little Behrooz in charge of a government post and with a government "stamp" with which he would clear drivers for trucks who were transporting foodstuffs from throughout Iran, in order to destroy the surplus of foods which would if they had been allowed to saturate the market place influence the economy in driving the costs of foods down encouraging market competition (which is something that the Shah was discouraging, because many of the clerics owned the farmlands and he was making solid attempts to modernize Iran and stop the negative influences of clerics authority over the people. Later in this book I will include additional

ETHEL C. RICHARD
with Dr. Antonio Gellini

information on the religious and political climate in Iran during the days of the White Revolution and the Shah of Iran's Iranian national reforms).

Little Behrooz had been given authority to maintain signatures, records of truck drivers and inventory, and being personally answerable to Mr. Khalatbari (this was the same Abbas Ali Khalatbari who also was General Secretary of CENTO (1962 - 1968) and who later rose into the position of Iran's Minister of Foreign Affairs (1971—1978) who had trained Behrooz to do this work daily after his classes), the records he'd submitted being kept and sent through his own father Mohammad Djalili who turned over the records to Mr. Khalatbari periodically—the same Mr. Abbas Ali Khalatbari who had told Behrooz that he, as an officer of the Shah, was accepting a position offered to him out of the country, (Ambassador to France) and who had told Behrooz (before he'd left Iran) that he was leaving him "in charge" of the government stamp (and therefore of controlling the disposal (and dispersal) of foodstuffs which provided for directing government food trucks throughout Iran, in the transport of those foodstuffs under authority of the King.

Therefore he'd left Behrooz in charge of a government post though still a very young child and believing that he would do a good job and that his father, who had been instructed to do so, would send to him the records which were turned over by Behrooz on regular basis ...he did this as ongoing training for Behrooz into a "higher" position planned for him as he got older. Of course, little Behrooz

ANTONIO GELLINI
Portrait of a Hollywood Legend

could not have understood or have known the seriousness of those powers that were in play within his young life, for he was being raised as the son of a diplomat who was an adviser to the Shah of Iran and also, was being raised during the years of the "White Revolution" wherein his actions within the capacity with which he was entrusted would carry a much heavier weight than his young five year old mind could fathom (and which actions he would decide to take in that capacity would directly impact the lives of the people of Iran (1965 -1973)and have a far reaching effect. This is a story which you will always remember both with smiles and with tears… and we have just brushed the surface of as much deeper story.

These events taking place prior to the Iranian Revolution (which happened during 1978), and those things which Behrooz would learn and those issues and values which he would hold dear to his heart would become challenged as he grew into a young man and discovered the meaning for his own life, and as he observed the struggle of his people and the turning of the tides of what had been multi-culturalism within his beloved Iran, witnessing the resulting outcome involving the aftermath of the Shah's exile and then in the knowledge of the execution by Khomeini's regime of the very man who himself had trained him in service to the King (April 11, 1979) among other heartbreaks. The world could crumble all around him however young Behrooz grew and became strong in personal character and knowledge and never forgot the meaning of caring and of family and of crossing

ETHEL C. RICHARD
with Dr. Antonio Gellini

borders in love for diverse cultures.

We start this biography with important information into the Shah of Iran, Iran's political climate of the day and the nature of those conditions which existed both before and upon the depose of the Shah of Iran by Khomeini, amid prosecutions of the Shahs families, friends and associates, Behrooz and his family of necessity had then also to survive prosecution.

Behrooz's father is a secular Muslim just as the Shah had been, and though Behrooz had attended the Islamic holidays and basic prayer as a young child with his father, his mom and grandmother are Jewish and Behrooz grew up to practice the Jewish faith (which in secular Iran of the 60's and 70's was quite normal and reasonable as many faiths intermingled and intermarried with no prejudice as is often seen in America today). Behrooz had been taught by his dad to respect and honor his mother, grandmother and all women. All throughout Iran in those days there was a huge diversity of religions and a rich culture of arts, and the Shah had been implementing reforms to better the lives of persons throughout his country.

The following is an short excerpt from an article which is available online from TheNewAmerican.com

ANTONIO GELLINI
Portrait of a Hollywood Legend

Meet the Shah

Tuesday, 12 May 2009 - Written by James Perloff

From 1941 until 1979, Iran was ruled by a constitutional monarchy under Mohammad Reza Pahlavi, Iran's Shah (king).

Although Iran, also called Persia, was the world's oldest empire, dating back 2,500 years, by 1900 it was floundering. Bandits dominated the land; literacy was one percent; and women, under archaic Islamic dictates, had no rights.

The Shah changed all this. Primarily by using oil-generated wealth, he modernized the nation. He built rural roads, postal services, libraries, and electrical installations. He constructed dams to irrigate Iran's arid land, making the country 90-percent self-sufficient in food production. He established colleges and universities, and at his own expense, set up an educational foundation to train students for Iran's future.

To encourage independent cultivation, the Shah donated 500,000 Crown acres to 25,000 farmers. During 1978, his last full year in power, the average Iranian earned $2,540, compared to $160 25 years earlier. Iran had full employment, requiring foreign workers. The national currency was stable for 15 years, inspiring French economist André Piettre to call Iran a country of "growth without inflation." Although Iran was the world's second largest oil exporter, the Shah planned construction of 18 nuclear power plants. He built an Olympic sports complex and applied to host the 1988 Olympics (an honor eventually assigned Seoul), an achievement unthinkable for other Middle East

ETHEL C. RICHARD
with Dr. Antonio Gellini

nations.

Long regarded as a U.S. ally, the Shah was pro-Western and anti-communist, and he was aware that he posed the main barrier to Soviet ambitions in the Middle East. As distinguished foreign-affairs analyst Hilaire du Berrier noted: "He determined to make Iran ... capable of blocking a Russian advance until the West should realize to what extent her own interests were threatened and come to his aid.... It necessitated an army of 250,000 men." The Shah's air force ranked among the world's five best. A voice for stability within the Middle East itself, he favored peace with Israel and supplied the beleaguered state with oil.

On the home front, the Shah protected minorities and permitted non-Muslims to practice their faiths. "All faith," he wrote, "imposes respect upon the beholder." The Shah also brought Iran into the 20th century by granting women equal rights. This was not to accommodate feminism, but to end archaic brutalization.

Yet, at the height of Iran's prosperity, the Shah suddenly became the target of an ignoble campaign led by U.S. and British foreign policy makers. Bolstered by slander in the Western press, these forces, along with Soviet-inspired communist insurgents, and mullahs opposing the Shah's progressiveness, combined to face him with overwhelming opposition. In three years he went from vibrant monarch to exile (on January 16, 1979), and ultimately death, while Iran fell to Ayatollah Khomeini's terror. Houchang Nahavandi, one of the Shah's ministers and closest advisers, reveals in his book The Last Shah of Iran: "We now know that the idea of deposing the Shah was broached continually, from the

ANTONIO GELLINI
Portrait of a Hollywood Legend

mid-seventies on, in the National Security Council in Washington, by Henry Kissinger, whom the Shah thought of as a firm friend."

Here is some further information on the climate in Iran during the Iranian Revolution of 1979 through the approximately 10 years that followed and I recommend you read their book as well.

From the book titled ***Blood & Oil: A Prince's Memoir of Iran, from the Shah to the Ayatollah*** by Manucher Farmanfarmaian and Roxane Farmanfarmaian.

I didn't stay long. Khodadad fiddled with his hands. Although he didn't say anything specific, I knew it was farewell. I didn't begrudge him his silence. You didn't escape alive by telling everyone your plans. Later, when I heard he'd left that same day, it came as no surprise. I was also thinking of leaving. Already I'd had a couple of close calls. The noose around the family was tightening. The regime was closing in, picking us off one at a time. Alinaghi and Eskandar were already languishing behind bars, poor devils. Alinaghi had practiced the anti-Islamic art of banking—charging people interest on their money. Eskandar had served the Shah as minister of the environment. How long would it be before it was my turn as an ex-director of the National Iranian Oil Company or worse, an ambassador, a personal representative of His Imperial Majesty? Already my minister of

ETHEL C. RICHARD
with Dr. Antonio Gellini

foreign affairs, Abbas Ali Kalatbari, a gentle man who had filled the post for twelve years, had been executed. In the month's right after the revolution, Khomeini had published a list of traitors to the state. Ministers, generals, prominent members of the great families, tribal leaders and a few big businessmen were all specified by name. Not so the Farnanfarmaians. There were too many of us. Rather than enumerate us one by one, -the list referred to us simply—and devastatingly as "the family of." In one sweep of the pen, all of us, born or unborn, were damned, our bank accounts flagged for seizure, our properties claimed in perpetuity by the revolution. Barred from appearing before a notary public or appealing to a judge, we could neither sell a car nor register a marriage. Any baby born into the family would come into the world without birth certificate or right to property.

The Shah who had been an ally of America and had been dedicated to improvement of life for Iran's citizens was gone. The Shah who had stood for equality, modernization and human rights for all Iranians and who had been strongly opposed by the Ayatollah Khomeini, who had pressed for Sharia rule against the monarchy, had won...

One little boy...Behrooz

We pick up the story here of Dr. Antonio Gellini, (Behrooz Djalili), son of Mohammad Reza Djalili who is now retired and is a highly respected professor of law, economics, religion and middle east politics. A well-known renowned

ANTONIO GELLINI
Portrait of a Hollywood Legend

political scientist, his father has authored very many highly regarded influential books and articles. What many have not known is the close relationship which was shared between Abbas Ali Khalatbari, Mohammad Reza Djalili and his son Behrooz Djalili while he was still a child which figures solidly within Dr. Gellini's life story. This is the story of Antonio Gellini, who was born as Behrooz Djalili in Mashhad, Iranian on April 24, 1958 and whose family was also very seriously impacted by the exile of the Shah and the takeover of Iran by the infamous Ayatollah Khomeini. Dr. Antonio Gellini is an international ambassador just as his father was before him. He is a United Nations ambassador for world peace and he is the Founder and Chairman of the renowned World Film Institute.

Behrooz Djalili's father was a diplomat (a foreign ambassador) for the Shah, and he and his close friend Abbas Ali Khalatbari had been directly involved in Iranian humanitarian efforts for the Shah, Mohammad Reza Pahlavi. Behrooz father having been an Iranian ambassador to several nations (his wife serving Iran at his side) and Behrooz as a boy had visited many foreign countries on holidays with his parents. Behrooz father was also a former classmate, close friend and personal adviser to the Shah, and therefore our very young Behrooz was treated as an "extended family member"(how else can I express it?) whose father and closest companions were already working in service to the King, and he (Behrooz) was being raised for high future position within his cabinet.

ETHEL C. RICHARD
with Dr. Antonio Gellini

Having come from such a past as stated above, when during his life as a very young boy, he did not assume that his life was strange, and young Behrooz Djalili, would attend his father's wishes, while as children do dreaming and thinking what he would personally would like to do with his life (even as a young child he thought about his own future). Behrooz loved movies and after his morning classes at grade school had ended and he was during late mornings being shuttled by a driver to his father's offices at Tehran University, he was dreaming of being an adult and about creating a worldwide "Olympics of Movies" in his free time after taking minutes and notes of meetings among professors within his father's offices at the University of Tehran where his father was then Chancellor.

These are the beginnings of the true behind the scenes personal life story of our much loved founder and Chairman of The World Film Institute, Dr. Antonio Gellini, when he was the little boy living in Iran whose name was Behrooz Djalili, and whose childhood was remarkable, and not only to his own personal life and history, but remarkable to the history of Iran itself, (and to the world—who up till now never knew his background or understood his influence while he was a youngster—nor that of the influence of his family) as he'd kept all a secret until the publishing of this, his memoir, and I am privileged and humbled to be his mouthpiece through this his commissioned biography. All of our readers are in for a heck of a special ride through the pages of Behrooz Jalili's

ANTONIO GELLINI
Portrait of a Hollywood Legend

life—(and to learn of parts of the Iranian story which occurred behind the scenes and which were never told) from the firsthand memory and perspective of one of the sons of the Shah's circle of friends and advisers.

And so it is, that we publish something very valuable for the knowledge of the people, straight forward and worthy of the man himself, the true untold story of Dr. Antonio Gellini and of the unknown factors which led to unrest in Iran, the Iranian Revolution of 1978 and the true beginnings of the renowned World Film Institute. I've promised you all a few major surprises and Dr. Gellini's life story carries more than a few.

I will do my best to outline the attitudes of the culture as I write for you about the personal side of Antonio Gellini, in which his attitudes are highly influenced and affected by his lifelong faith as well as by his upbringing within the Iranian Culture of his childhood, the influence of his parents (often times he is heard to give greatly deserved honors to his mother), as well as his life and experiences up until and during the Iranian Revolution.

Coming from a background of severe almost incomprehensible traumas, it is Dr. Gellini's faith, his belief in having heart for others and in encouraging charity and love for others, maintaining family values, honoring diversity of cultures and of the arts, that are at the heart and soul of everything he does. Truly it can be said of Dr, Antonio Gellini that he is here to fulfill one purpose, "To Help Unify the World for Lasting Peace, through the mediums of

45

ETHEL C. RICHARD
with Dr. Antonio Gellini

Cultures, Arts and Entertainment." And as he has often been heard to say, "Together we are making a better, safer world for our families...our men, women and our children."

*Mohammad-Reza DJALILI/
Member of Scientific Council

Mr. Djalili holds a Doctorate in Political and Diplomatic Sciences from Université Libre de Bruxelles (ULB), Belgium; He was Professor at Graduate Institutes of International Studies and Development Studies, Geneva, Switzerland. Dr. Djalili is researcher and world-renowned scholar specialized on contemporary Iran, Conflicts in the Middle East and on the Geopolitics of Central Asia and the Caucasus. His publications include among others: Géopolitique de la nouvelle Asie centrale : de la fin de l'URSS à l'après 11-septembre [Transl. "Geopolitics of New Central Asia: from the USSR's end to Post-9/11"] (PUF Publisher, Paris, 2003), Géopolitique de l'Iran [Transl. "Geopolitics of Iran"] (Complexe Publisher, Paris, 2005), Histoire de l'Iran contemporain [Transl. "History of Contemporary Iran"] (La Découverte Publisher, Paris, 2010), Les Relations internationales [Transl. "International Relations"] (PUF Publisher, Paris, 2012), L'Iran et la Turquie face aux 'printemps arabes' [Transl. "Iran and Turkey faced with 'Arab Springs'"] (GRIP Publisher, Bruxelles, 2012). Mohammad-Reza Djalili , born in Tehran

ANTONIO GELLINI
Portrait of a Hollywood Legend

on September 22 , 1940, Of Swiss nationality [ref. needed] and Iran, is a doctor of political science and diplomacy of the Free University of Brussels , Professor Emeritus Institute of International and Development Studies in Geneva (Graduate Institute, Geneva). He taught in the 1980s at the University Paris II. Professor at the Faculty of Law and Political Science of the University of Tehran in the 1970s. He also served approximately four years as chancellor for the University during the White Revolution beginning in 1962-1963 school years.

THE PROCESS

I ran into the usual problems we run into with doing an immigrant American's bio, which are difficulties with matching dates and names, which in reality are many times often changed or misspelled in birth certificates and other documents. Since I was not an expert on Iranian history I've had to research quite a lot of it and I pray that I have included enough of it here that our readers will have realistic depiction of actual events of that period in which Dr. Gellini grew up. Though many did not escape, there were persons who were involved with the Shah's government who were forced into exile from Iran during the period of the Iranian Revolution.

Those who have been forced into exile from other countries have been at times given documents which hide former identities, and there are those persons whom come from foreign nations to the United States, Canada and European countries, from nations where often times births were not recorded properly but were left to the memory of the elders. Let's not forget that we are talking about a man who spent his youth in the middle of and being deeply entrenched within influences of the Shah's reign during the years just preceding the Iranian Revolution of 1978 and the

ETHEL C. RICHARD
with Dr. Antonio Gellini

takeover of Iran by the Ayatollah Khomeini February 11, 1979. That young Behrooz had to deal with those same circumstances as all young Iranians had, but from the perspective of being the son of one of Iran's national class member families of that time. This would mean that anything and everything which he did would be noticed and would reflect the image of the Shah himself and of his father and his friends, as his father held a position as a working member of the Shahs government as did others within his circle.

Ayatollah Khomeini was ruthless and many friends and family were persecuted, many killed and those who made it out were forced into exile and I am certain that it is for these reasons why Dr. Gellini has kept these facts of his biography a secret for all these many years. Dr. Gellini has also experienced profound inexplicable tragedy within his own personal life, and taken together these events which led to his founding of The World Film Institute coincided with these and necessitated his inner struggle towards resurrecting within his own heart a balance of healthy determination to improve—not just his own—but other persons prospects for a brighter outcome of life, though they also had suffered, through the encouraging of healthy cultural activity and a wholesome happier environment for families, and especially for women and children through film and the arts.

Though his father had wanted him to become strictly a lawyer or a doctor and his mother had encouraged him in the arts and film as she had expressed to him often that he should, always follow after the desires of his heart.

ANTONIO GELLINI
Portrait of a Hollywood Legend

In a sense he did follow within his father's footsteps as well because today he is an honored world renowned United Nations Ambassador for Peace (awarded by WCH International and the Universal Peace Federation) working as founder and chairman through the World Film Institute's Olympia Awards Competitions of Cultures, Arts and Entertainment encouraging international business exchange in the arts and entertainment field under UNESCO supported projects and organizations, and he regularly meets with presidents of nations and high level dignitaries from all around the world and is involved in high level peace projects which bring nations together to further the cause of international cooperation to help bridge cultures and foster a better understanding between peoples of the nations.

Dr. Gellini though many do not realize it, on a more personal level is normally a quiet, private and shy man. I have noticed this while speaking with him and through watching some of his older taped interviews where he has helped himself to combat his shyness issues though prepared speeches which, though they come from his heart (he's prepared them himself) they also avoid any hints of his long ago past, histories of his families background, the lingering grief and battle of emotions.

Dr. Gellini is upbeat and friendly when facing a crowd however behind closed doors the sadness of a horrific past, being raised as a child in Iran during the Pahlavi reign and the White Revolution, and having survived the Iranian Revolution, and having participated as an officer involved in Iranian economic reforms himself, (being appointed to a

ETHEL C. RICHARD
with Dr. Antonio Gellini

government post even as a young boy) and being himself a child raised to take a high position within the Shah's cabinet, his life had been marred by serious tragedy and upheaval at every corner of his childhood. It is my job to bring his story to you and it is not a task without tears. I have felt the pain right along with him as we went over very seriously emotional memories, issues which only the very strong of heart and mentality can handle without breakdown. Dr. Gellini has had no ordinary childhood or young adulthood.

It has been my privilege by which I am humbled that he has allowed me many interviews of both historical and personal nature and I have taken the confidence that he has placed in me with great seriousness of responsibility. It is my determination that the bio which I am presenting within this book is both accurate and sensitive and able to meet full standards of respectability and it is my prayer that many will come to understand the heart of the man and the very important message which this true story holds for all of the nations and that perhaps the publishing of this biography will be of some serious real help toward the goals of World Peace which we would hope to make great strides within during our present generations.

The current generation of Americans does not remember as we older Americans do the reputation of Mohammad Reza Shah Pahlavi, The Shah of Iran who was thought of as insensitive, ruthlessly westernized and hard on then Iranian clerics, which were born in Iran and who preferred traditional Islam and Sharia government over an American or European ideal, and though the Shah's was Shia, he held more lenient

ANTONIO GELLINI
Portrait of a Hollywood Legend

secular ideals which included the modernization and economic growth of Iran (which his father Reza Shah Pahlavi had started before him) and he had shown some success, however he had encouraged a pull away from hijab, had instituted a westernized dress code, voting rights for women and a policy for better education urging literacy and the arts, which the Ayatollah and other clerics considered a heresy and an evil westernization of the country, …and the Shah was known for confiscating properties and criticism of the clerics (whom complained to media), and the people of Iran being drawn into the argument and eventually siding in majority with the Ayatollah (including students) because of the Shahs poor planning in that he was moving the country in the direction of an western ideal, which many people could not fathom, and he had included land reform and economics which had raised many eyebrows (henceforth the resulting rage of the religious) and so that they considered him a traitor to Islam, and were resentful that the Shah himself would consider himself to be above the law of Sharia.

The Shah taking lands and funds from the clerics (those who felt that they were who really ruled Iran and that the Shah must obey Sharia law) for nationalization and redistribution to private use, which was creating great inconvenience to the clerics as their lands were being taken and was considered against the Islamic Constitution, which imposed upon the monarch that the clerics and Sharia be obeyed by both the monarch and the people. The Shah, who had a reputation for fairness toward every segment of Iranian

ETHEL C. RICHARD
with Dr. Antonio Gellini

society had fought against the influence of the Ayatollah Khomeini, and the clerics who'd spoken against him, and the Shah exiling Khomeini.

The Shah had taken monies from oil sales and confiscating from these other sources, had created a Iranian reforms package where he was building roads, hospitals and instituting secular government offices and improving schools. All of this created further resentment with clerics who then influenced the people and therefore, they banded against the Shah because of what they saw were hardships brought against Iran's religious families as a result of the Shah's policies.

While in a desperate attempt to secure his country with the help of the American government, FBI and SAVAK, during his reign the Shah was falsely accused of criminal activity with propaganda being issued by Iranian clerics of he having committed crimes against God and the nation, assassinations, arrests and the murders of protesting students, all of which however falsified served to incite the people.

The Shah, who had been supported by America and countries around the world as the legitimate ruler of Iran, who had been justly imprisoning criminal elements within Iran (who were clerics, members of the religious right who were committing crimes against the people and then attributing their crimes to the Shah) and working hard to bring better living conditions to the people, though not justly deserving of it, had earned for himself amongst the Ayatollahs and fundamentalist Imams and of his own people,—the reputation of an traitorous, self-indulgent and murderous dictator who was set to destroy

ANTONIO GELLINI
Portrait of a Hollywood Legend

(Islamic ideals of) the Iranian state.

The Shah and the Royal family were finally exiled, fleeing under threat of death by the returning Ayatollah Khomeini (during 1978), taking refuge within several nations until finally into Egypt, where the Shah passed away in 1980; and later, Royal family members became removed to the United States, to Boston and to New York City and to Los Angeles and where a few are today still living within the Los Angeles, California area.

"*In the end, he was a man without a country. Forced to flee the gathering storm of revolution in Iran in January 1979, the shah, his wife, Farah, members of his family and a dwindling retinue of aides and bodyguards moved from one country to another in search of a secure asylum. They went first to Egypt, then to Morocco, the Bahamas and Mexico. On Oct. 22, 1979, he came to the United States for a gall bladder operation and treatment of cancer. Thirteen days later, militant Iranian Moslems invaded the U.S. Embassy in Tehran and took Americans there hostage to demand the shah's extradition, the return of his wealth and a U.S. confession of "crimes" in Iran. At the end of the shah's medical treatment in New York, Mexico refused to allow him to return. He went to Panama and then again to Egypt. He died of complications from his cancer treatment yesterday at the Maadi Military Hospital in Cairo. He was 60.*"—From, The Washington Post, Deposed Shah Dies in Egyptian Exile By William Branigin July 28, 1980.

History remembers the hostage crisis takeover of the American embassy in Iran during the year following the

ETHEL C. RICHARD
with Dr. Antonio Gellini

expulsion of the Shah where originally 66 American diplomats and citizens were held hostage for 444 days from November 4, 1979, to January 20, 1981 after a group of Iranian students belonging to the Muslim Student Followers of the Imam's Line, who supported the Iranian Revolution, took over the U.S. Embassy in Tehran. Fifty two of the original 66 persons were held hostage in Iran during the tenure of President Jimmy Carter.

The Shahs family has been saddened through tragedy upon tragedy and we show respect and add our hearts and our prayers to the memory of those who grieve and are among us.

This biography is correctly set to begin within the reality of what were the years of the White Revolution and into and through the Iranian Revolution, for this is the backdrop from where the child Behrooz Djalili sprang. Behrooz Djalili was destined to become in later years an American whose name is Dr. Antonio Gellini, and whose destiny as an United Nations Ambassador for World Peace remains to affect good throughout the entire world by his presence within it.

There are some facts of Dr. Gellini's life of which we were not made aware. We will now continue in our exploration of the good hearted Iranian American man who found himself working to assist other good hearted people and families of the world, in working for legislation supporting rights for families in healthy entertainment, and in working toward understanding and peace between people of diverse cultures and nations—after himself having survived the long standing issues of his own country and of his past.

MY YOUTH

*"When something comes from your heart
and you always want good for other people…"*

*"From the age of five I was so busy. I
would not ever live in Mashhad again and I
continued my life in Tehran…"*

Little Behrooz at five years old was put into a car and his driver would deliver him from his classes at grade school to his father's offices which were inside the University of Tehran where his father was Chancellor (1963). He would sit with his dad among the professors of Tehran University during meetings, watching people come in and going out while learning what was being done there, and practicing to write through taking notes—and therefore was the little person of five years old taking official memorandum notes (which was job as he was instructed to do by his father) so that they would all remember what was discussed as subject matter the previous session of that week …he would call it off when again the meetings would convene the following week …and then little Behrooz would during the meetings take more notes.

Behrooz had been moved to Tehran in stages, first into his aunts home where he stayed for some eight months and his

ETHEL C. RICHARD
with Dr. Antonio Gellini

parents had been very busy with work and not often able to have him with them, and so he was later moved from his aunts home and back in with his parents for a short time and then was put into the care of others, he lived with a nanny (from Russia) and two maids, one from China, another from Taiwan. Behrooz loved to study and also he loved the arts, and especially movies, and every chance he got he would fantasize and think about making movies and about how wonderful it would be if there were an "Olympics" with awards that would only be for film. Also, Behrooz had a big dream even at five years old of becoming a movie actor and a director…

There wasn't time for playing with other kids, as Behrooz was expected to work hard every day to learn his studies where he attended school half days while being trained in the afternoons by his father to keep memorandum of meetings of the professors at the university and on weekends he was being trained to do inventory for the king, counting foodstuffs which were being dumped into the ocean outside of Iran off trucks. Behrooz completed his two years of studies as a very young boy within one year as he was a much focused boy who loved to obey his parents and his teachers.

By the time Behrooz was 5 years and eight months old he was left "in charge" of inventory of the contents of those food trucks, being given custody of a legal stamp and the authority of the Shah's government of Iran to allow the trucks to pass and to deliver their contents to their destination, getting each truck driver to "sign in" within his written records. It was *(Abbas Ali Khalatbari (his fathers close friend) who was head

ANTONIO GELLINI
Portrait of a Hollywood Legend

of economics for Iran who had given to Behrooz the job to count the foodstuffs which were being destroyed in 1963 during the years of the White Revolution, also known as the peaceful revolution and Iranian reforms.

One might ask how this can happen that such a young boy can be given such huge authority and responsibility of the government and the answer is simply that he was trusted to do his job and to hand over the records of the receipts and signatures of truck drivers to his father, who would then turn them in to his own friend, Dr. Khalatbari, whom Behrooz simply called "uncle." It was a private arrangement and his father (then President of Tehran University) along with his friend (* Abbas Ali Khalatbari)—had future plans for Behrooz and so they would train him in this way ... that they would give to him great responsibilities while he was still young, which were directly involved in actual Government business.

Behrooz was a young boy who was awestruck at the many beautiful forms of art from the diverse cultures that were on display in Iran while he was growing up. Gardens and fountains, beautiful scenes of architecture, people from differing backgrounds, religions and philosophies, poetry and dance and music, sculpture and theater of the time and the colorful sights and sounds of everyday life which pervaded the cities and the countryside of his native Iran. The Persian land was alive with personality of spirit and rich culture and Behrooz knew first hand their exquisite value as he looked upon and experienced the rich, delicious cultural activity, and it tickled his palate with an insatiable desire to inhale into his

ETHEL C. RICHARD
with Dr. Antonio Gellini

being every flavor of his fondest memories while being within his homeland. Behrooz whose dad was an Ambassador of Iran to France and other countries, of which I know Switzerland was a favorite, (his father having been born of both Swiss and Iranian heritage and today his parents reside there) during his young years was many times brought on trips to foreign countries with his parents and so Behrooz also had the rich and rare opportunity to experience these firsthand as well.

*Abbas Ali Khalatbari (1912 – 11 April 1979) was an Iranian diplomat, who served as the minister of foreign affairs from 1971 to 1978. Khalatbari was a career diplomat.[6] He was among the significant diplomats who shaped the foreign relations of Iran under the reign of Mohammad Reza Pahlavi. [3] He began his career in finance ministry in 1940 and then joined the foreign ministry in 1942.[5] He briefly served as the Iran's ambassador to Poland in 1961.[5] He was appointed secretary general of CENTO in January 1962, replacing Mirza Osman Ali Baig in the post.[7][8] Khalatbari was in office until January 1968 when Turgut Menemencioglu succeeded him in the post.[9] From 1968 to 1970 he served as the deputy minister of foreign affairs.[10] Khalatbari was appointed foreign minister in 1971, replacing Ardeshir Zahedi in the post. [1] Khalatbari paid an official visit to Israel in 1977 as a guest of his Israeli counterpart Yigal Allon.[11] Khalatbari's term as foreign minister ended on 27 August 1978[12] and he was replaced by Amir Khosrow Afshar in the post

Behrooz started working with his father at the age of five years...

ANTONIO GELLINI
Portrait of a Hollywood Legend

"When I was about five and a half years old a family member, (who was in charge of and managing the economy of Iran) brought my father and I south of Iran and I was talking with one uncle when I saw a big truck that had a lot of rice and they were dumping it all into the ocean, and they had a lot of beans, and were dumping it into the ocean, and so I asked, "Uncle, why are they using rice for feeding the fish?" He answered me, "no, no, no… you do not understand son. I give you an example, the rice sells for one dollar a pound, and with so much rice going into the cities, it will break their price and if you break their price it's not good for the economy."

So, he trained me for this job many months and then I started at age 5 years and 8 months in being solely in charge of keeping tally on the bags of rice and beans, roasts and other different things that were being dumped into the ocean off the coast… I wrote all of it down as that was my job. Then after some time went by, one day my mother introduced me to one movie which I loved very much and is named Miracle in Milano—and watching the movie I saw poor people (and they were really very poor) and it was such a great story and there was a theme to the movie about poor people winning at a lottery system by ticket (and the winners would receive chickens and money and luxury) and so, after seeing it one day I asked the driver of our car if there were anything like that in Iran for poor people …and he was sharp with me in his answer, and that he was too busy to talk with me and he had a lot of paperwork to complete, …and so I was very sad

ETHEL C. RICHARD
with Dr. Antonio Gellini

and I did not feel comfortable.

When he stopped the car I wrote down the name of the town and addresses and so I had enough records—and then one day on the ride back home my uncle said, "I am going to France, because we have more business now" (he had become higher in position for Iran and was going to France for a celebration), he continued "...and you will come here and everything in the trucks you will write it down and your father will send the records of receipts to me."

I'd read a letter then explaining my duties and I could see what my job entailed and that if I wanted to and the drivers had my authority stamp that they could keep a part of the food and that I could also stop food from being loaded into the ocean to be destroyed—and so to try it out I gave the local address I'd collected during my training to a driver and he brought the food where I'd told him, and later again one each to a truck driver of where to send food (to each a different place in a town or city) and when it worked, and I knew that the truck drivers would go where I would tell them, I thought to myself, "hey, this works and I can be feeding a lot of poor people in all of the country" and so I sent more trucks out to feed all of the poor people, and just like in the movie, Miracle in Milano, it worked and everything that the drivers had to go into the ocean—I gave it to the poor people of the cities and towns throughout Iran.

During those years while I was doing this I attended a school called Shah Abbas Armen High School which housed grades K-10 as was standard practice within Iran then and

ANTONIO GELLINI
Portrait of a Hollywood Legend

which continues today. During those years for me I saw what was happening around me however I was concentrating on school and my job and I lived as a very busy young man. My family would sometimes bring me on holiday with them and all together I had 12 international trips with family while I was growing up and before my 17th birthday.

I was still in my thirteenth year when I had passed my university admittance exams (called Concour) and I was then admitted into Tehran University, the youngest person then in history of the school to be admitted, and I was small of stature, and being so young I was treated as a kind of role model for other students in schools throughout Iran, with my photo in newspapers and magazines, and the Minister of Arts and Culture were setting up personal appearances for me in different cities of Iran. So I'd had status as the youngest person at the University of Tehran and as I have said, I was absent at times in order to travel throughout the area as well as abroad with my family. From the years of five and 8 months to thirteen years old I'd been left with a nanny and household servants in Tehran while my mother and father had worked together for the Shah outside of the country.

On the day I am speaking of, when I was thirteen and I was waiting for my limo while I was at the school and waiting for Mrs. Parsa (Minister of Education for Iran) to take me to the airplane (because I was going to Isfahan, Iran). I remember that I saw my photo on a magazine cover on a stand and when I looked up from it and about 10 feet away from me I saw two young people from the university who

ETHEL C. RICHARD
with Dr. Antonio Gellini

were playing leap frog and I had a strange feeling that I could not describe.

It came to me that I was sad and something felt wrong inside of me, because I had never really had a childhood and I did not know as they did, how to "play" and so my ego was shattered—and where normally I would write a note to my father and to others at the university, this time I didn't do that and something felt very uneasy and sad in my heart. After I arrived in Isfahan and at the Abbasi Hotel, I would stay all night till early morning five o'clock and then I had to go with the officer.

The officer who greeted me was Minister of Cultures, (Mr. Mehrdad Pahlbod), and he approached me and acting very playful, said, "Hello, hello! You know, you are the youngest student ever to be admitted to Tehran University? ...and we are very proud of you! Thank you, thank you! Can you walk with me?" I walked into the hotel with him and he was behaving oddly as if he were joking with me and so I thought that he was funny but I was a little confused because in a way it almost seemed to me as if he were laughing at me.

I was not a child anymore (because I was thirteen years old), but the way he'd behaved made me somewhat interested in getting back to my childhood, and so when I went back home to Tehran I started becoming interested in and becoming involved with studying wrestling and later upon the urging of a person from a local soccer group I started playing soccer. I also began boxing as I'd read about and I'd

ANTONIO GELLINI
Portrait of a Hollywood Legend

become a fan of Muhamad Ali. All of these sports I was trying out, because I was just learning how to play. I always tell everyone that kids should be learning from six, seven and eight years old to play sports, however I'd not had the chance when very young and so at thirteen I was just beginning.

After I returned and I was back in school there were student groups who went around into different areas and towns playing soccer and I was asked to play, and when I did play scores were usually in our favor and so one day I was asked to play at the front of the team and I had refused, telling the coach that I wanted to play from the rear instead. There were some ten thousand people watching us play that day and I remember that the ball came to my feet and then "go, go, go, and crash, crash and pow!" I kicked it to the goal! All of the people got suddenly very quiet—everybody stopped talking and nobody was clapping and so I was thinking that I did something wrong…and then the people were all exited within the studio and some team player came up to me and said to me," 'What happened?…you kicked the ball under and passed me instead of kicking it to me and that is not usually done in our Soccer! You kicked so strong and came from all the way in back and I didn't even get a chance to kick the ball because you had nailed it." So in Soccer I finished in that day as number one, and that was the end of my soccer playing days for me and my family.

You know I really liked Muhammad Ali and so I studied everything I could get my hands on in order to be good as he was so that I could also be a village favorite and that year we

ETHEL C. RICHARD
with Dr. Antonio Gellini

had a big wrestling show and matches which many celebrities attended that took place with students coming from Tehran University. I was thirteen years old and still I was doing a good job sending out the trucks to feed the poor people, and did not dump food into the ocean and nobody knew.

I went to the wrestling matches with my mom which had 20, 000 people attending, and the youngest people from the schools were wrestling that day with 48 celebrity wrestlers and we had as a referee—the famous Hossein Mollaghasemi—and there were many people present who had come to watch the wrestling matches that day, including the Shah's brother. The founder of the wrestling matches announced that the King's brother and some others from the palace were there to watch the farmers wrestle.

There was a famous wrestler there who was wrestling with young people in a team's wrestling exhibition and so I was watching what was going on in that corner. I saw him wrestling with another young person and some people started talking with me and telling me that, "if you want to wrestle then you have to watch and you have to learn by doing it" The Icon took up three numbers and didn't give them to the man he'd just fought. Finally later his team went to approach the Icon to wrestle and so they allowed the match and the crowd started throwing cucumbers, apples and things at me—can you imagine 20, 000 apples being thrown at me?

They were booing and saying, "What? Can you win?!" I said, "What happened? What are you doing?" (We have to believe and to pass to other people—and you see that

ANTONIO GELLINI
Portrait of a Hollywood Legend

wrestling taught me this). Anyway, of all things the King voted a request that I had to after this match was finished present the award, to hold up the trophy to the winner. I went over there and I don't know what happened, but the first minute I put that trophy down I'd knocked him out.

Everybody just came and being proud. I picked up the man and I hugged him to myself and all the crowd didn't know what to think. People were shouting, "give him (meaning me) the gold!" I did not accept it. I gave it to the icon. Everybody was upset, and I said, "No. I am not wrestling today, I'm sick of wrestling!" ...and I walked away from this wrestling.

On the way back home from the university that day my mother told me that my King and my father had spoken together because the King found out that instead of doing my job that I had been giving away everything, all of the food to poor farmers and village people all throughout Iran, and for eight years...and then my mom asked me, "What happened?" (The King had been made very upset because many people had been aroused when it was found out that the food was stopped from being delivered to them).

What had happened was that I'd been called away to make appearances and my first stop had been Isfahan and I could no longer do my weekend job (because I was traveling) and so a new person had been placed in that job—and Mr. Khalatbari had checked up with him in order to make sure that he was working his job properly, and the new person who was using my records had been continuing to do what I

ETHEL C. RICHARD
with Dr. Antonio Gellini

had been doing (because of course he'd been given my records) and when he got a follow up visit meant to simply check up on things that's when uncle Abbas found out that I had been sending the food trucks out into differing cities and villages in order to feed the poor people of Iran and that the food was not being destroyed as he'd ordered me to do, and that this had been going on for eight years. Mom was also very upset with having received the news.

FOUND OUT
The SAVAK Investigation

I got the call while I was at Esfahan from SAVAK asking me to return to Tehran so that they could talk with me. My dad also called and asked me if I were okay (I was still just 13 years old). When I arrived at SAVAK I was asked many questions over and over again for a rather extended period (3 hours). They found out that I'd been giving food to the poor for eight years. The food I had been sending out had been stopped from being shipped to those persons, and the SAVAK officers wanted to know where I'd gotten the idea to give away the food, who told me to do it, instead of having destroyed it as I'd been instructed to do by Dr. Khalatbari.

I explained to the men that I'd seen the movie years before (when I was five years old) called Miracle in Milano and that I had wanted to help poor people too just like in the movie—and that this was how I got the idea. The officers pressed me further for three hours straight, repeatedly asking me about my parents, Dr. Khalatbari and other officers (both in and outside the military). The officer explained to me that his talk with me was confidential, that what I had done had aroused the people and that he wanted to know the truth and

ETHEL C. RICHARD
with Dr. Antonio Gellini

that it was SAVAK policy to ask me to speak the truth.

I explained it over and over again that I had watched the movie, Miracle in Milano and had prayed about what I could do to help poor people. I saw that I had the control of the stamp and that I could do it and so I decided myself that I would do something. I was asked what were my motivations for having disobeyed my orders in the giving away of the food, and I replied to the officer, "Love for the people from my heart."

I'd done a radio interview that following week and so people knew my story and what had basically happened, and my name was in the news.

A week later when the people throughout Iran saw that the food had been stopped, there starting at Mashhad, began an uprising in the cities, where food had been being dispersed and was no longer available. In Tehran, people were rioting and looting and had set out to burn down the palace, the result being that two days into the protests the Shah called a curfew on the third day for people to clear the streets by eight pm or else be immediately arrested. I went into the radio station, and I called the curfew myself asking the people to obey the curfew. When the people did not at first listen, the Shah called for the army and there was martial law called throughout the country at eight pm.

The information on what was happening was broadcast on the radio, and so everyone knew what everyone else was doing when this happened. I went into the radio station and I took the microphone. I addressed the people telling them,

ANTONIO GELLINI
Portrait of a Hollywood Legend

"This is Behrooz Djalili, and I want to apologize and to tell you that I love you and what I did for my people is because my King inspired me and that it was he who told me to do it. I would like for you all to calm down, stop rioting and to go home." Soon afterward there started what seemed to be a miracle. Precincts were calling into the station that people all throughout Iran were changing their attitudes, and started pitching in to repair the damage which had been done and hugged the army. In Tehran the news anchor at 10:08 pm started crying as he announced the good news and the people worked throughout the night to repair the damage that had been done.

Later, the king called my father to invite him and our whole family to the palace for dinner. He wanted to show his appreciation for me having spoken well of him over the radio. He'd said, "Your son saved my life, and I want to give him the best gift. So bring your son to the palace." So my father called and asked me to come back to Tehran, as I was visiting at the time of his call with my aunt (father's sister who lived in Mashhad). However, as it happened, I never got to attend the dinner. However, my aunt told me that she would be happy to bring me to the palace.

I remember he took me to my room. He came into my room and closed the door. I was very young, thirteen and a half and I would never dare to touch my aunt, and he beat me very badly and all my body was in pain and bleeding and with a lot of blood. During the beating I could not cry because there was too much blood... and (they) were also

ETHEL C. RICHARD
with Dr. Antonio Gellini

beating my aunt. I fell down thinking, *what happened?...* I said, "remember, you are just one man!"

My aunt crying, and I started jihad (to struggle). I was trying to ask him to fix my body, and I said, "...my brother" and he said, "...not *my brother's* job! That was the King's job!" You are wrong and we want to give you a gift because you are wrong!" He said. "Now focus on your lessons from the culture and how it is important."

I was brought to the hospital to heal and the King and his son came to visit with me at the hospital and they made sure that I got good medical care over the following few months.

COMING TO AMERICA

Thoughts About the World Film Institute & My Marriage with an Angel Whom I will never forget

My major in college was history which focused on diversity of cultures, of peoples and religions, sociology and political sciences. I pretty much kept to myself focusing on my studies and I was not involved with social or political groups. I would observe what went on within the streets and consider ways in which I might become a teacher of sorts, an influence and an inspiration to others for good, that perhaps I might through my life help some poor wayward soul to find his or her way through life with less emotional difficulty, hardship and loneliness. I looked for ways to integrate adapting these ideas within my scripts for both the theater and for films.

I'd married during my eighteenth year and fresh out of school and I'd married a lady from one of the greatest, one of the finest noble families of Lorestan Province. My wife Parvin was a lovely, fine lady with a great vision and who always loved to help people. She cared about families and children and was the first to pitch in and assist when someone needed a helping hand.

ETHEL C. RICHARD
with Dr. Antonio Gellini

My first film was titled GRADAB (RIVER) and it was a drama about two students, one which was living a wholesome life of good attitude and eager to learn, of good character—and the other character in the drama was a troubled youth who was addicted to drugs and who was challenged about the meaning of life and about his own self-worth. The film ended with the troubled boy becoming so inspired by his friendship with the other young man that he sought help, quitting his drug habit. I had been creating films and showing them in Tehran University Theater, and often times I would bring the films into the public forum outside of school. My films were always with a theme which might teach a moral precept or make an inspirational statement or which would encourage love and good relationships within families and emphasized good education.

The Film RIVER was never to be licensed within Iran because of internal politics within the country (because of the Iranian Revolution) however, later it was shown in Europe. The first film festival I'd ever attended was marked by tragedy however, as I had attended the Tashkan, Russia Film Festival in order to pick up my award, and while I was away from home I got the call that my lovely wife, her sister and my brother in law who were back in Iran had been in an auto accident and that my wife and her sister had not survived. It was 1979 and I was twenty one years old and with two precious baby daughters to think about. I was devastated and I returned home with a very heavy heart. With so much sadness, grief overwhelming

ANTONIO GELLINI
Portrait of a Hollywood Legend

me at that time everything else having happened in my life and suddenly my life and that of my daughters was changed in an instant and it was very hard to deal with, however I had to seriously decide what would happen with my daughters. My beautiful daughter's... By the grace of G-d their lovely and kind grand mom (my wife's mother) took in my children Sanaz and Elham the eldest just three years old and she assisted me to raise them from that point on, providing them each a stable home and I visited with them every chance I got.

I first came to America during 1981 and though my goals involved directing and making films I saw a need within my new community for an Iranian establishment, as there really wasn't anything available in the area for Persian people and I wanted to further knowledge within the community of the Persian culture. During that same year I returned to Iran for a short time in order to purchase books. I obtained 28,000 books—varying forms of Persian literature, poetry, religions, philosophy, etc. I returned to America and set up first a book store and I established a poetry night.

Later on into it (during 1985) I set up a tea room and a restaurant where we also served Persian cuisine. We were open for business at that same location for seven years and during 1992 through 1994 I took English as a second language at the Evans Community School at the corner of Sunset Boulevard and Figueroa. On vacations and other occasions I would visit with my family and would sometimes attend international film festivals, and making known my

ETHEL C. RICHARD
with Dr. Antonio Gellini

plans for establishing film schools and a world film awards competition. I founded the World Film Institute as an educational establishment and founded an awards platform to assist new artists and to encourage diversity in film, incorporating differing films from many cultures.

EPILOGUE

Dr. Gellini is one of the fortunate ones to have come out of the Iranian Revolution with his life intact (taking into account his family associations and friendships with those of the Shahs high officials). So if he feels that he is somehow chosen for some lofty calling in life this may well be the case, as those who understand the devastation created by the illegal acts and crimes against humanity committed by Ayatollah Khomeini and his regime totally destroyed the lives of thousands of good people, men, women and children who were the families of the former Shah and of his officials within his cabinet and others who had held civil offices, school officials and teachers, postal workers, doctors and their families as well as all business people and bank officials who'd dealt with westernized companies and had worked to help modernize the country in several areas of development, all throughout Iran. The regime executed a death sentence on everyone who'd been found to have sold western clothing to females as well on anyone who had taken out a loan from a bank. Secular businesses were shut down, their owners imprisoned and later killed, their families who could make it out alive were in exile and their

ETHEL C. RICHARD
with Dr. Antonio Gellini

lands and properties confiscated.

Dr. Gellini's parents had been out of the country during the revolution and he'd stayed behind and was low key while working within the theater at the university at Tehran creating plays, directing and acting within film. Since he'd been young and appeared to be a student in school and had not been an obvious opponent to the Ayatollah, having taken no political position and having stayed away from such groups and had seemed agreeably quiet and not a threat he was skipped over when the Ayatollah's regime did their sweeps looking for those who were acting officials of the former Shah's monarchy. At that time he was twenty one years old and he had set his mind on film making.

But a film maker who respects true education and who encourages peace and acceptance between people of diverse cultures was not going to be successful within Iran with the Ayatollah now in charge of the nation and with so many of Dr. Gellini's associates having been imprisoned and executed - Dr. Gellini knew better. Khamenei refused to abide by any humanitarian rules whatsoever and Dr. Gellini knew he had to leave Iran in order to be happy and to work and to complete his personal life's mission. He had planned to come to America even before he'd left school because he believed that there is very much opportunity within America to live out one's life with right freedoms and to make a good life for one's self.

He came to America with a dream within his heart and a

ANTONIO GELLINI
Portrait of a Hollywood Legend

goal to establish a school to teach others in film and also in order to make films that were also able to educate and inspire others toward serious meritorious humanitarian and family causes. Dr. Gellini has always been an activist for, and in the encouraging of healthy competition, and for wholesome family and children's entertainment.

PART TWO

THE UNTOLD STORY OF ANTONIO GELLINI
Portrait of a Hollywood Icon

These days, on the world stage of arts and entertainment not everyone is a major player for positive change and as a matter of fact there are those who would disintegrate what arts that are, which the unappreciative would dare destroy. Within these ill fitted times unappreciative souls give little thought that perhaps the God of our universe in the wise forming of man from the dust of the earth and breathing into him an enlightened spirit, that it is through persons of heart wherein which God Himself lives and would have it be that humans enjoy a stroll down blooming roads or within one of our museums of antiquity or perhaps through a garden full of unique landscape and natural sculpture—silhouetted amid the living creation's fragrant blooms, viewing exquisite paintings hung within a gallery—or that by eternal design within the music of a dance lays magic and that even the birds chirp the melody of the arts!

Here among the powers that be many today have lost sight of those most precious ubiquitous pleasures and so

ETHEL C. RICHARD
with Dr. Antonio Gellini

there had to enter upon this unique structure of events in time a man whose curiosity and love for the world, purity of heart and caring for his fellows would come on the scene. A man so connected to the source of life's energy, wherein the seat of personality (the mind) meets with the seat of spirituality (the heart) which within the human species transforms that inner bond into philosophy and art so as to make it impossible to deny that even the Creator would enjoy the menagerie of ancient as well as modern arts and all forms of healthy entertainment, that as a facet of human personality are an expression of the divine spark within each person, which are extended within the giving and entwinement of all nations coming together.

So onto this stage of universal human endeavor of expression in the arts walks Antonio Gellini, a man of simple lifestyle, high spiritual standards for dignity, moral stature (and) a family oriented individual who's heart rests with children and families. Born in Tehran, Iran and being the son of a diplomat from an very early age he visited many countries with his family and because of this he'd been exposed to many cultures (both within and outside of Iran) he having visited 23 countries. When 17 years old he decided to take action upon the advice of his mother, and Dr. Gellini opted to follow his heart into the field of arts and entertainment, and not to become a lawyer or a doctor, as were his father's wishes. Following a career path first as an young actor and not too long afterward, into film making, the young Antonio was inspired by the huge

ANTONIO GELLINI
Portrait of a Hollywood Legend

diversity of many cultures and was fascinated with them, wishing to help bridge cultural differences which he saw between nations and while at the same time to help bring a broad enrichment to persons of all cultures through the expansion of, and exposure to, international arts within several countries.

He first began his career within the internationally known film festivals. He created films of an activist nature which earned for him some serious respect as a spokesman within that venue and while doing so he also had set out to create an awards program with the focus in his mind on a world film awards competition which would be based upon the framework of the existing World Olympics of Sports. The concept and program of today's internationally acclaimed and backed Olympia Awards of Cultures, Arts and Entertainment began with this formula which during those days were being thought out in detail by a young Antonio during Dr. Gellini's early career and which were central to his heart in the forming of an international arts and entertainment inter-cultural program and movement in order to help bridge nations differences bringing people of the world together for enlightenment, unity and peace.

In the mid 1980's he would move to Los Angeles in the United States, open an Iranian bookstore, later adding on a family café and a fitness room in the Iranian sector of the city while in his spare time he would network and be active within film circles and would go on to found The World Film Institute, and down the line from there he would

ETHEL C. RICHARD
with Dr. Antonio Gellini

become one of the worlds most beloved icons of the 90's in his own right and within the formation of an historic partnership with the legendary Dick Clark and Dick Clark Productions.

A Cozy Iranian Cafe in Westwood

February 05, 1989 | CHARLES PERRY
A "Fair Use" excerpt from the LA Times

"Snuggle in the Cozy Restaurant," says its business card. Whole families are here at 11 p.m. on Saturday, from grandmothers in scarfs to babes in arms. Some, though surely not the families with small children, will stay until the 4 a.m. closing time.

The Cozy Restaurant was once open around the clock. Owner Bruce Djalili says he only cut back the hours because he's so busy these days trying to break into Hollywood.

The Cozy Restaurant is not as wild or crowded as this most of the time, though, because the singer-dancer (who also tells a million jokes in Farsi) only performs Thursday through Saturday. Most nights a smaller audience comes to hear Iranian pop songs and the sobbing, melodramatic, highly embellished improvisations of Persian classical music, played on either of two sorts of long-necked lute.

And during the day, from 10 a.m. until the music starts 12 hours later, it's usually quiet. There will be just a few people who come to eat or chat and drink glass after stubby glass of tea.

The Cozy is right down in "Persian Gulch," that stretch of Westwood Boulevard from Santa Monica to Wilshire where a lot

ETHEL C. RICHARD
with Dr. Antonio Gellini

of Iranian restaurants and shops are found, both because of the Iranian students at UCLA and the numerous Iranian families living in the neighborhood.

It gets an upscale Iranian crowd anyway; the late Shah's brother has had a birthday party here. The music may have something to do with it, but there are also foods that can't be found elsewhere.

You would certainly have to come for dizi. The restaurant's name may be Cozy in English, but in Farsi the sign out front says Dizi, after the house specialty. Dizi a dish of lamb, potatoes, beans, some tomato paste and aromatic preserved lime peel stewed together for seven hours.

Owner Bruce Jalili, who looks a like a younger, cuter Michael Nouri, is an authentic self-starter. He first opened a wholesale Iranian book store in this location four years ago. Then he started having readings by Iranian and Afghani poets on Tuesday nights then tripled the size of the place and put in a kitchen and bingo, it was a nightclub.

While plunging into Hollywood (there's a photo of him with Sly Stallone on the wall), Jalili is sticking with the Cozy, and working to reinforce his Iranian heritage. He's starting a new Iranian theater, and he plans to open a zur-khaneh , a sort of gymnasium where you work out not to Jane Fonda tapes but to recitations from the Iranian national epic.

ANTONIO GELLINI
Portrait of a Hollywood Legend

Like everyone else in L.A., of course, he has written a screenplay. It's titled "How to Survive in America." It does not, however, include the recipe for dizi.

Cozy Restaurant, was located at 1781 Westwood Blvd., Los Angeles, was Open for lunch and dinner from 10 a.m. to 4 a.m. daily.

LET'S FORGET THE POMP OF HOLLYWOOD

For a moment let's focus on the man, (and his many important and valuable accomplishments) for this is about one young man's act of love for family and for his fellows around the world. He is spiritually centered and one who loves people and puts his heart on the line every day in order to affect some hope within the world for healthy endeavors in cultural competition, wholesome family entertainment and a healthier environment in order to raise our children.

During 1994 Antonio had already had some success with a couple of his films and one in particular known as Berlin Wall. One day while Antonio was present with Jack Valenti (President of the Motion Picture Association of America) while he was staying at the Majestic Hotel, Cannes Film Festival, (France) they'd had a conversation together in which Jack had expressed how much he'd liked Antonio's film Berlin Wall. When Antonio had answered that he'd not come to discuss Berlin Wall, Jack asked him, "Why did you come?"

Antonio explained how he had an idea that if the festivals all each agreed to give to the winners of their festivals a final competition at the world stage level which he titled, "The World Film Awards" that it will be an great

ETHEL C. RICHARD
with Dr. Antonio Gellini

incentive for international artists to present their work and to be acknowledged as the ultimate winner and the world's finest within the field. Jack was very excited about Antonio's idea and told him to return again the following day when he would present this idea to the crowds, which there were to be at least 1,000 participating festival artists and some 50 directors present.

Toward the following evening Jack took the microphone and addressed the crowd, "we have been here 10 days and everyone attacks one another arguing over winners place but I have good news for you...Antonio has a program for World Film Awards. Work with him and Hollywood will look for you! So, then that it will be the winners of the Cannes, Berlin and all other important film festivals will compete together for a solution!

In private, Jack addressed his new friend Antonio saying to him, "Come to the United States and I will introduce you to Mr. Dick Clark!"

So Antonio returned to Los Angeles and to Jack Valenti in Burbank who introduced him to Dick Clark and his wife and to Gene Weed who would be producer and director for the at that time future Family Film Awards television show. Jack took Antonio aside and exclaimed, "Why didn't I come up with this idea? Antonio, this will be your office! (and he got for Antonio both his office and his parking space, gave to him money to start work and also a deal with Ted Turner (of Turner Broadcasting Company) and in an exclusive front page article within the papers it was publicized that The

ANTONIO GELLINI
Portrait of a Hollywood Legend

World Film Awards were to go on the air November 21st, 1995 (after the Venice, Italy Film Festival).

After the news hit the papers about a new World Film Awards many artists were very exited about it and who were invited to the Hollywood Oscars of 1994 began to cheer for the World Film Awards and Antonio had also been invited to the Oscars and in his excitement in getting to the awards show he had been driving, was nervous and he had an accident on the way to the show. He ended up arriving at the Oscars in a taxi and with his face cut and bleeding and it was Sofia Loren, Ted Turner and Stephen Spielberg's wife who greeted him and helped him to clean up before the show.

Clint Eastwood and many others were cheering on for the World Film Awards and not for the Oscars and the television studios executives who had a huge stake in the Oscars, and which were also present began to panic as they were concerned that a World Film Award would take away the viewership and the sponsors for their yearly Hollywood Oscars.

Later, Antonio received notice that he was being sued by the studios in order to stop his World Film Awards for which he had a contract to produce with Ted Turner from becoming a television awards show. Judge Harold Greene (famous for having divested the monopoly of AT&T) was presiding the day that Antonio was scheduled to answer the suit n a Los Angeles Federal Court. When the judge told Antonio that he had an option to obtain a lawyer Antonio insisted that he would defend his own case and then he proceeded in his own defense. .

ETHEL C. RICHARD
with Dr. Antonio Gellini

Antonio insisted the World Film Awards were not a matter of money but were a matter of education and that he was not seeking the studios money but that as an American citizen who loves America he would give the money back to American citizens out of love for his country, because America had treated him with open arms and had been very good to him. The judge then gave to Antonio a hug, told him that he had the right of countersuit and expressed to him that he is a good man, while also proclaiming that The World Film Institute is a legal entity of public education in the film arts. Antonio did not pursue lawsuits against the studios because he has a strong cultural background which opposes such things as lawsuits, he having being born in Iran where the prevailing belief is that in order to be a good person one must appreciate his country and it's people and to be grateful, and not to pursue money unearned or to be greedy.

Antonio also has a tremendous heart for families and for healthy children's television programing and he has been of serious help to push out the stench of mental illness which has over past years crept into the film and television industry and which left without restraints would threaten the simplicity, purity and innocence of family entertainment. Though the world rants loudly on the subjects of racial, ethnic and gender inequality none have actually participated to the extent within the film industry and with an activist spirit to effect long term positive change which benefit children and families through their advocacy as has Dr. Antonio Gellini.

ANTONIO GELLINI
Portrait of a Hollywood Legend

Much of what we perceive as "wholesome" within family entertainment today is a direct result of Dr. Gellini's intervention within this staggering multi-billion dollar film and entertainments industry that we call Hollywood, which in fact is more a euphemism for a certain mindset than a place. Aside from a sidewalk where one can view "stars" names or for a museum of Hollywood memorabilia or some famous hot spot location of yesteryear (such as a famous television studios backlot) Hollywood is a fictitious location for a manufactured image play land of glamour and of big spenders. ...that which many a young person's fantasy revolves around (and which of course in fact can never be acquired with happiness attached), however which many a studio big shot of the past has sought to capitalize on (this image of the Hollywood royalty) in harmful, uncaring ways, and simply in greed to make a dollar. Hollywood had also in those days monopolized the major film festivals around the world (back in 1994) and entertainment was becoming a cesspool of violence and sexual content unfit for families and the influence of the studios leaving no room for competition of independent or cultural and international films within the worlds festivals or within the world market. Family films were also not the sought after norm and big bucks murky waters ruled.

One day while walking on a beach and thinking Antonio happened upon a magazine stand and his attention was drawn to a particular magazine cover which boasted a photo of a statue of the Virgin Mary with hands

ETHEL C. RICHARD
with Dr. Antonio Gellini

outstretched. He felt led, being a spiritually minded man, to pray. He had been thinking about his friend Dick Clark (who was not feeling well and who'd had a stroke and about people in general and he had been very dismayed at the current movies of the day, that they were so bad for children. He then placed a phone call to his friend Jack Valenti (then president for the Motion Picture Association of America) and went to visit with him for a talk. It was at that time Antonio presented an argument to Jack that studios were making 900 movies a year but there was no push or incentive to make family films and that outside of the Disney Company families and children were becoming very much ignored in the industry. Antonio and Jack Valenti decided that Jack would get Antonio a conference with then President Bill Clinton who was to appear at a fundraiser soon within the Center Plaza Hotel at Los Angeles.

Jack and Antonio went to the fundraiser together and Antonio did have that conference with Bill Clinton, during which it was said by the president, "How is it that Antonio Gellini, who has come from another county, has come here to help America!" … and so it was during April of 1995 when a new law was passed which would guarantee that each studio must release at least three family films each year. It was during that time when The World Film Institute (Antonio Gellini) created The Family Film Awards and along with his new partner Dick Clark (Dick Clark Productions) began production plans for the Family Film Awards yearly (there

ANTONIO GELLINI
Portrait of a Hollywood Legend

was to become a five year contract) television show which would start as a two hour special and catapult excellence in the film industry for family film producers, directors and artists into the national and cultural spotlight for recognition. The Stanley Morgan Advertising Company who had been sifting through other shows which were all possibilities for the primetime two hour slot and were in competition for the lineup on CBS that season had come TO Antonio with an offer saying that all looked good for the Special and that he had gotten ATT to sponsor The Family Film Awards Special on the CBS network. The five year contract with Dick Clark Productions now included a five year contract with CBS and which included 5 year option. Here is some additional information for our readers to better help you understand the situation in place with the studios back during the latter 80's and into the 1990's, and including statements made by then President Bill Clinton during his inaugural speech which addressed the issues then within the entertainment industry. You will also find a letter presented to Antonio Gellini (founder of The World Film Institute) written then to congratulate him on his new Family Film Awards Television Special which aired on the CBS network August 22, 1996.

A STATEMENT MADE IN 1996 BY A *PEOPLE MAGAZINE* CORRESPONDENT:

"The budget ceiling for African-American productions is dramatically lower than for so-called mainstream projects," says Warrington Hudlin, who has produced four of his brother Reginald's movies. Hudlin cites their experience after their first studio film, House Party, grossed over 10 times its $2.5 million budget. "One would think that the interpretation would be, 'Here are guys who have their ears to the ground, so let them come back with a more challenging budget to make even more money,' " he says."But instead the response was, 'No, you'll do another movie in the same budget range.'

Part of the studios' justification, Hudlin says, is their contention that "blacks don't sell overseas." Yet he points out that Eddie Murphy's 1988 movie Coming to America, made for $39 million with a virtually all-black cast, did a whopping $350 million internationally. And last year's Bad Boys, starring the lesser-known Will Smith and Martin Lawrence, scored $75 million overseas. (Its U.S. take was $64 million.) "There's conventional wisdom that catches on," Hudlin says. "Statistics come out that refute it, but people hold on to it."

Current wisdom also says that things have never been better for black actors. They "are having a field day," says one who is, three-time Oscar nominee Morgan Freeman. "I don't think Hollywood is racist; I think Hollywood lives and dies on greed. Jobs are not given because of race. They're predicated completely on money."

ANTONIO GELLINI
Portrait of a Hollywood Legend

It is not hard to glean from the above information that Hollywood was manipulating the world film market, and held the monopoly on films, and films festivals around the world.

FROM *THE LOS ANGELES TIMES*
Hollywood Money Blunts Clinton's Barbs: Politics: President treads carefully in critique of industry. Unlike Dole, he does not lay blame for eroding values primarily on popular culture.
June 19, 1995 - JOHN M. BRODER and DWIGHT MORRIS
TIMES STAFF WRITERS

WASHINGTON – *After Senate Majority Leader Bob Dole (R-Kan.) unleashed his recent attack on Hollywood, President Clinton hastened to proclaim his own credentials as a spokesman for American virtue against the depredations of the entertainment industry. For example, in the 1992 election cycle, Time Warner Inc., the media giant singled out by Dole as purveyor of some of America's most depraved music, and its executives gave more than twice as much money ($1.49 million) to Clinton, other Democratic candidates and the party itself as the entertainment industry as a whole gave to Republicans ($640,000).*

Hollywood money has been a mainstay of Democratic campaigns for years, and top industry officials have been among Clinton's most generous sponsors. "Overall money figures show that Hollywood favors Democrats by overwhelming margins: For the 1992 elections, 86% of the money given by the entertainment industry through political action committees or individual contributions went to Democrats; in 1994, in the face of strong Republican challenges to congressional Democrats,

ETHEL C. RICHARD
with Dr. Antonio Gellini

the number rose slightly to 87%.

White House officials say Hollywood's generosity to the Democrats makes Clinton's criticism of the industry that much more courageous. "It's easy to criticize those who will never support you anyway, as Dole did. But what takes courage is to say these things to your friends, as Clinton has done with violence and Hollywood," said Rahm Emanuel, the White House director of special projects who has frequent contacts with entertainment industry figures.

The White House aides point to a consistent Clinton record of chastising Hollywood for what he called in this year's State of the Union Address "the incessant, repetitive, mindless violence and irresponsible conduct" portrayed in movies, television and music.

So, having been fed up with the Hollywood Film Industry monopoly of the day back in 1995, when Antonio Gellini hit the scene he sought to bring the monopoly down and his effectiveness is one of legend, as he single handedly formed the process which forced the industry to make policies, which upon his activism with his arrival initiated the demand for more films of G and PG ratings to be produced by film studios, (and thanks to his association and friendship with Jack Valeni (then President of the Motion Picture Association of America) and a meeting of Dr. Gellini with him and President Bill Clinton, who were in agreement with him) and put these new regulations into effect creating within law a clause providing that the film studios must make at least three family oriented feature films per year which created and maintained a real value

ANTONIO GELLINI
Portrait of a Hollywood Legend

for these films within the industry, and then, Dr. Gellini, by instituting an awards platform (which came into being shortly thereafter, and a highly rated very successful television awards show which was produced by Dick Clark Productions in conjunction with its creator Antonio Gellini and The World Film Institute and which was titled the Family Film Awards. Antonio was co-executive producer for the Family Film Awards Television Special of August 1996.

The Family Film Awards still exist for family oriented entertainment and which are meant to bridge the gaps between studios, for creating a kind of cooperation between studios, encouraging through healthy competition the making of better, healthy family and children's films through honoring top producers, directors and actors of the industry for excellence in the making of family films. Later when the studios attempted to take Dr. Gellini to court in an effort to stop him in continuation of using the trade names "Family Film Awards" and "World Film Awards" in conjunction and partnership with Dick Clark Productions the famous Judge Green determined that Dr. Gellini has full rights to his logo and the created names for his projects, including that of the use of the name Dick Clark Productions and of the original Awards Show and its various identifications.

ETHEL C. RICHARD
with Dr. Antonio Gellini

THE WHITE HOUSE

WASHINGTON

August 7, 1996

Warm greetings to everyone gathered in Los Angeles for the premier Family Film Awards, presented by the World Film Institute. I am delighted to join you in congratulating all the nominees for their outstanding contributions to family entertainment.

The ability of the United States to make the twenty-first century the age of greatest possibility in our history depends in no small measure on our ability to build strong families today; to help parents succeed not only in the workplace, but also in their most important job -- raising good, well-educated, well-balanced children. Because films, television, and music are such influential forces in the lives and education of our children, we have been working hard to give families real choices in the quality of their children's entertainment.

The entertainment industry is making an important contribution to this endeavor, as is reflected in these first-ever Family Film Awards. The artists and productions you honor at this ceremony have shown not only a strong dedication to excellence in their art, but also a genuine commitment to communicating the values we work so hard to teach our children: compassion, self-respect, responsibility for their actions, and the courage to stand up for their beliefs. You have proven that films, music, and television can be inspiring as well as entertaining, educational as well as commercially successful.

On behalf of America's families, I thank you for your vision and leadership. Let us continue to work together to build a future bright with promise for our children.

Hillary joins me in sending best wishes for a memorable evening.

Bill Clinton

ANTONIO GELLINI
Portrait of a Hollywood Legend

THE WHITE HOUSE
Washington DC - August 7, 1996

Warm greetings to everyone gathered in Los Angeles for the premier Family Film Awards, presented by the World Film Institute. I am delighted to join you in congratulating all the nominees for their outstanding contributions to family entertainment.

The ability of the United States to make the twenty-first century the age of greatest possibility in our history depends in no small measure on our ability to build strong families today; to help parents succeed not only in the workplace, but also in their most important job--raising good, well-educated well-balanced children. Because films, television, and music are such influential forces in the lives and education of our children, we have been working hard to give families real choices in the quality of their children's entertainment.

The entertainment industry is making an important contribution to this endeavor, as is reflected in these first ever Family Film Awards. The artists and productions you honor at this ceremony have shown not only a strong dedication to excellence in their art, but also a genuine commitment to compassion, self-respect, responsibility for their actions, and the courage to stand up for their beliefs. You have proven that films, music, and television can be inspiring as well as entertaining, educational as well as commercially successful.

On behalf of America's families, I thank you for your vision and leadership. Let us continue to work together to build a future bright with promise for our children.

Hillary joins me in sending the best wishes for a memorable evening.

-Bill Clinton

ETHEL C. RICHARD
with Dr. Antonio Gellini

The viewership for the original television special was through the roof with over 7 million viewers and was the most viewed show on television in America of all the networks the night it aired. Things looked great for the future of the Family Film Awards. However Dick's health began to decline and Antonio who loved Dick like a brother and who did not want to continue the show without him held out hoping that Dick would recover from his illness and that they could resume work together.

Everyone who was an important actor or superstar in Hollywood stepped up to the plate wanting to work with Antonio and to host the show until Dick could return to work. Robin Williams, Eddie Murphy, and others lined up to try and convince Antonio to continue the yearly Family Film Awards Shows, however Antonio was too despondent and said no to CBS and even to Dick himself out of respect for his (Dick's) position as his partner.

Antonio, who did not want to work with anyone other than Dick Clark, and was of the opinion that if Dick could not be part of The Family Film Awards then it would be too highly disrespectful and disloyal to Dick to replace him as Dick was not only Antonio's partner, he was also his close friend. So, in Antonio's opinion since it was Dick who had worked with him and he had a contract with Dick Clark Productions that it was morally wrong to cancel that contract and to invite another company's contract in for the purpose to continue the shows without Dick Clark Productions, and that it would be a very serious insult to his friend, whom he loved, for him to do so.

So, in following his heart, in many ways Antonio Gellini has preserved both his culture and his integrity.

THE OLYMPICS OF THE CULTURES, THE WORLD'S BEST OF ARTS AND ENTERTAINMENT

The Dawning Of World Olympia Awards Competitions of Cultures, Arts and Entertainment

Dr. Gellini has not only been involved within these processes and within other projects of magnitude, his success at what originally were impossible odds has proved to be phenomenal. What started in the early years with a (by itself phenomenal) friendship with and the backing of Jack Valleni, which led then to friendship and partnership with the iconic Dick Clark, and Dick Clark Productions, Joel Diamond and Gene Weed and which led also to the historic Family Film Awards of 1996, Antonio as founder of The World Film Institute has himself became an icon of American history and a force to be reckoned with in his deeply rooted desire for the original intent of his heart, which has always been to further the cause of culture and the arts throughout the world with the instituting of his concept of a World Olympia of Cultures, Arts and Entertainment to coincide with the Worldwide Olympics of Sports.

That his dream has been successfully implemented into existence and is now a viable Olympics of Cultures, Arts and

ETHEL C. RICHARD
with Dr. Antonio Gellini

Entertainment and is honorably positioned and supported by many countries, their dignitaries and heads of state, is a true testament to the man of heart at its helm). Taking this story further, where did it in reality all start and what can be gleaned from the even deeper personal, untold story of this legendary, humble and caring human being? Much has been published about Antonio Gellini and each story written has sought to get at the essence of who he is, where he came from and his spiritual roots.

I wanted to get at something even deeper than these, which is "what creates this kind of unfailing spirit in a man that he can continue in these endeavors and without resentment at the maltreatment he has himself experienced upon the cancellation of the World Film institute (and Dick Clark Productions) contract (s) with Ted Turner in 1995 when the studios, (looking to nix him and his World Film Awards Shows contract, (which would have propelled World Film Awards (then a project on the table and planned to air in August of 1995) into the stratosphere, had it become reality at that time. In second thoughts for the contract, the studios had filed lawsuit against The World Film Institute and Dick Clark Productions, they not wanting competition with their own Oscars Awards shows) they bought out rights from Ted Turner, making Ted Turner chairman of Time -Warner (and therefore making him a studios puppet) effectively cutting the World Film Institute and Dick Clark Productions off from further participation in production of World Film Awards Shows.

ANTONIO GELLINI
Portrait of a Hollywood Legend

You see Dr. Gellini who had every right and reason to sue under the circumstances, still he chose not to sue ...and then because of a series of challenges, first at the loss of the production of the annual Family Film Awards (which was Dick's end of the cancelled contract) and then with the failing health of Dick Clark (which led to he eventually succumbing to his illness), Mr. Gellini out of respect for his friend and partner had put aside his most heartfelt personal ambitions for The World Film Institute's World Film Awards and The Olympia Awards of Cultures, Arts and Entertainment, (his pet idea and dream since childhood and which is now in existence and a true Olympics Competitions created to help bring unity and peace between cultures and nations of the world) and the Family Film Awards got temporarily put on a back burner as well.

These were heart wrenching decisions at the very least of it. Ten years went by since the passing of Dick Clark before Antonio Gellini would reenter the scene making important headway in the forming of partnership with the highly respected, heart driven and himself iconic Allan Jay Friedman.

The World Film Institute and Antonio Gellini its founder and chairman, and Allan Jay Friedman once again would become a household name and the World Film Awards would become an integrated part of The World Olympia Awards Competitions of Cultures, Arts and Entertainment—12 Olympias—in the category of Film; creating, under the direction of Antonio Gellini and Allan Jay Friedman, a NEW World Olympia reality.

ETHEL C. RICHARD
with Dr. Antonio Gellini

Antonio Gellini has created at least 175 Arts and Entertainment Awards and has the approval and sponsorship of many nations and we know that this is no small feat for any man to accomplish single handedly, or even with others hands helping in the effort. Today we can happily report that Dr. Gellini's message and work to promote world peace through the medium of international cultural competitions and cultural exchange in arts and entertainment has reached into and touched the hearts of the heads of many world governments. China, South Korea, the Philippines, Ireland, United States, Sweden, Africa and France and others have all come into the program. Dr. Gellini is a United Nations Ambassador for International Peace through the arts which is a diplomatic position awarded by United Nations participating humanitarian programs promoted under We Care for Humanity, and the Universal Peace Federation in cooperation with UNESCO.

ANTONIO GELLINI AND COMPOSER AND AWARD WINNING PRODUCER ALAN JAY FRIEDMAN
From an article by Maurice Dwayne Smith, Cold Heat News, 2014

Antonio Gellini, founded not only The World Film Institute, The Family Film Awards, The Olympic Arts, and The Olympia Awards, which is the first award system to be awarded to the best films from a competition comprised of all major film festivals across the world, and President Allen Jay Friedman, were recently honored, via Princess Maria Amor's, in New York

ANTONIO GELLINI
Portrait of a Hollywood Legend

City, in The United Nations Building, at her 2nd Annual G.O.D. Awards, which is becoming an international barometer of a dignitaries', or performer's success. He said that it will consist of a talent pool of 250 and a panel of respectable and notable entertainment experts and film critics will choose the top three choices from among fifteen different categories.

Mr. Gellini expounded on his view of the role of artist in the world today by saying, "In these changing times, where the creation of visual images throughout the world can be shared through powerful mediums that cut across all boundaries, I believe that we as filmmakers have an important responsibility because what we do can affect the entire world. We can eliminate the barriers of race, age, gender and religion through visual stories that take viewers on an adventure or impart information. From India to Chile to China and even Hollywood, film touches one and all. I congratulate all who create art and images. I especially congratulate the Family Film Award and Olympia Award nominees in the past, and all those who will be nominated in the future. Your influence on the world is amazing and has the incredible power for change."

Antonio Gellin's Family Film Awards are given to films that are family oriented and are G and PG. Such notables as Sandra Bullock, Ron Howard, Steven Spielberg, and Clint Eastwood have passed through The family Film Awards circles and Antonio is not letting up in his quest to take films and send it around the world touching and changing hearts and minds for peace as best he can. In fact, Dr. Gellini was awarded The Ambassador for Peace Award last summer.

United Nations Messengers of Peace/Goodwill Ambassadors are distinguished individuals, carefully selected from the fields of art, literature, science, entertainment, sports or other fields of public life, who have agreed to help focus worldwide attention on the work of the United Nations. Backed by the highest honor

ETHEL C. RICHARD
with Dr. Antonio Gellini

bestowed by the Secretary-General on a global citizen, these prominent personalities volunteer their time, talent and passion to raise awareness of United Nations efforts to improve the lives of billions of people everywhere.

Appointment:

The United Nations Secretary-General appoints Messengers of Peace. Goodwill Ambassadors, on the other hand, are designated by the heads of United Nations Funds, Programs and specialized Agencies, e.g., UNICEF, the World Food Program (WFP) and UNHCR. Goodwill Ambassadors are subsequently endorsed by the Secretary-General.

Goodwill Ambassadors vs. Messengers of Peace:

Goodwill Ambassador Programs have been in place across the United Nations since 1953. They are designated by the heads of United Nations funds, programs and specialized agencies and are subsequently endorsed by the Secretary-General. Some agencies also use eminent personalities in other capacities, such as UNESCO, which has designated "Artists for Peace."

It is to Dr. Gellini's accomplishments which I as well as countless others applaud him for his vision and his commitment to further the cause of World Peace and Unity through these Olympia Award Competitions of Cultures, Arts and Entertainment and for his constantly holding close to his heart the values of family and of healthy family entertainment.

ANTONIO GELLINI
Portrait of a Hollywood Legend

In June 2014 Antonio Gellini was honored with the Ambassador for Peace Award

NEW YORK - Mr. Antonio Gellini, the founder of the Family Film Awards and Olympia Arts, and his partner, Multi-Award Winning Producer-Writer-Composer, Allan Jay Friedman, the President and CEO of both of these distinguished enterprises, were honored on June 20 at the (G.O.D.) Awards, presented by We Care For Humanity (WCH) in New York.

A banquet for 400 dignitaries from around the world embraced this historical event "to unite the world through peace, love, hope, and the arts, which is the basis of every great civilization," Friedman says.

ETHEL C. RICHARD
with Dr. Antonio Gellini

World Film Institute President Mr. Allan Jay Friedman was honored to give a speech at this historical event at the United Nations. Following is the excerpt of the speech:

ANTONIO GELLINI
Portrait of a Hollywood Legend

"In these days of stress, hate and corruption, have you ever dreamed of a united and peaceful world filled with love, hope and passion… an exalted world which is a safe, free and noble place for children, a place where dreams come true…where living is not a struggle but a joy! Of course you have…so has every human being since time began….always the same dream…some call it Shangri-La…others, Utopia, still others, Heaven. And, it is Antonio Gellini's, and my, dream to make this dream come true.

"Mr. Gellini and I feel it's time to bring God, who inspires our dreamers, artists and creators, back into our lives and to educate our hearts, where God lives, and not just our mind. It is a time to transform our unhappy world into a joyful heart-driven world instead of a mind-driven one.

"For, the dream is the only reality and Olympia Arts, which is the presenter of the Olympia Awards, is here to be the protector of the dream, which is reflected through the arts.

"It has taken a visionary from a far off land, rather than America, to recognize this important need. And, he has done it through Olympia Arts, which is the 'Olympics of the Arts.'

"Olympia Arts and the Olympia Awards which Antonio Gellini, the Founder of the Family Film Awards, created calls it a two week 'Celebration of the Spirit.'

"This 'Celebration of Spirit' will be done every three years, with several 2 hour TV specials and other events honoring each one of the best of the best from each of the many categories within the 12 arts: literature, painting, music, dancing, sculpturing, theater, film, men and women's martial arts, fashion design, culinary arts, special needs; and a Humanitarian Award for the most noble artist of all.

ETHEL C. RICHARD
with Dr. Antonio Gellini

Joel Diamond   Antonio Gellini   Ambassador
Rebecca Hadden   Mr Ben Lai
                            wife and Daughter

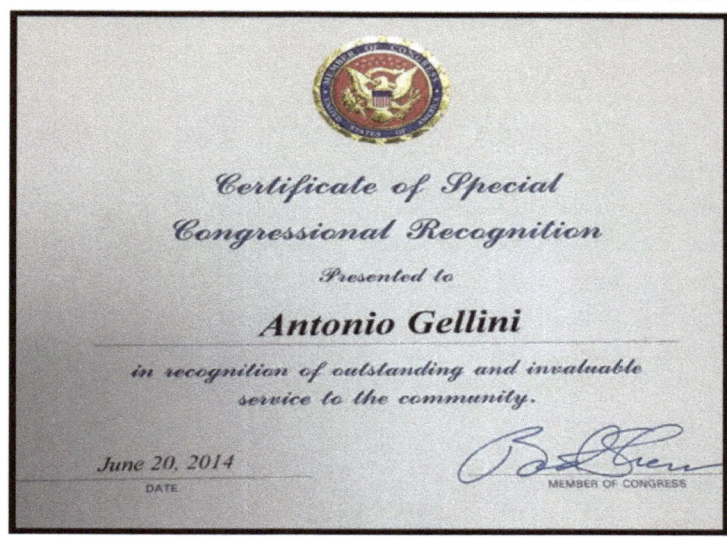

Certificate of Special Congressional Recognition

Presented to

Antonio Gellini

in recognition of outstanding and invaluable service to the community.

June 20, 2014
DATE   MEMBER OF CONGRESS

ANTONIO GELLINI
Portrait of a Hollywood Legend

"During this 2-week transcendent experience, there will be: 1. A one day "Symposium of Excellence." This will feature people from the different categories of the 12 arts. They will evolve the making of the "best" artists in the world. 2. A "Course of Legends" will be a one day entertainment seminar with the best of the best from each of the categories within the 12 Arts. They will reveal how they found and manifested their purpose-driven-destinies. And 3. Olympic Arts will be an Internet School featuring the best teachers in the world from each of the categories of the 12 Arts.

"These will be followed by a broad spectrum of already written theatrical musicals, concerts and movies created to educate, inspire, elevate and entertain.

"It is the mission of Olympia Arts to bring our world together through that which is the basis of every great civilization and which lives on long after we have all gone: the 12 Arts.

"And, it all begins with being heart-driven and not mind-driven and trusting our goose bumps (intuition), which is that whisper from God."

WCH Founder and President, HH Princess Maria Amor Torres, DD said, "This is one of the biggest collaborations in the history of philanthropy."

2nd Global Officials of Dignity Awards (G.O.D. Awards) is "the leading international awards honoring excellence of individuals who have outstanding civic, charitable stewardship and have significantly improved the quality of life in their communities through their expertise..." as stated on the G.O.D. Awards website.

ETHEL C. RICHARD
with Dr. Antonio Gellini

As Antonio has often stated, "Olympia Awards Competitions of Cultures, Arts and Entertainment are not mine and belong to the people."

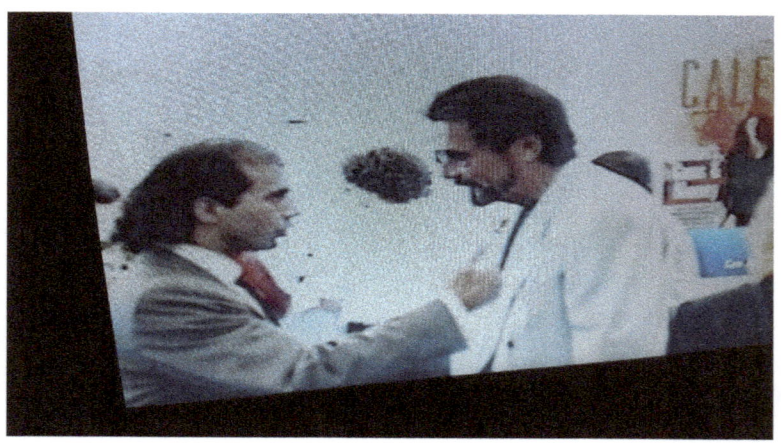

Antonio and James Brolin (1995) at the Moscow Film Festival

ANTONIO GELLINI
Portrait of a Hollywood Legend

DREAMCHASING & GLOBETROTTING

FOLLOWING the path of a 12 year dream, the **World Film Institute's** (WFI) existence and influence in the domestic and international marketplace today is a result of aggressive global efforts over the past 12 years. By targeting film festivals, film and television markets and events to promote its own concept, scholarships and awards programs, WFI has created unprecedented momentum in the areas of publicity, organizational support, and international festival support.

WFI's success is also a result of incredible timing. Starting its campaign on the heels of historic international changes and events has greatly influenced its conceptual acceptance. This new found "Global openness" will continue to grow and add further fuel to WFI's unique international appeal, flair and advantage.

The first bricks that were laid as the **World Film Institute's** "early foundation" did not come without great effort, dedication and, of course, an incredible amount of international **travel** by its Founder and President, **Antonio Gellini** and a very short list of others, including the faith and vision of Tichi Wilkerson Kassel. The following pictorial is a salute to those historic journeys and of course to the man behind the wheel.

Sylvester Stallone and Arthur M. Kassel

(l-r) Arthur M. Kassel, Antonio Gellini with Pierre Viot at the 1996 Cannes Film Festival

(l-r) Gene Weed, Joel Diamond, Antonio Gellini, Arthur M. Kassel and Dick Clark announcing the Family Film Award nominees

(l-r) Actor James Brolin chats with WFI Founder/President Antonio Gellini at the Moscow Film Festival

Antonio Gellini and Martin

(l-r) Mr. & Mrs. Gerard Yvos, General Manager of the Hotel Martinez in Cannes with Antonio Gellini and Arthur M. Kassel at the '96 Cannes Film Festival

ETHEL C. RICHARD
with Dr. Antonio Gellini

(l-r) Telecast Dinner Chairman Arthur M. Kassel, Stan Mogars, Gene Weed and Antonio Gellini

(l-r) Antonio Gellini flanked by Gregory Peck and Yani Begakis

(l-r) Beverly Hills Councilman Allan Alexander, Curley Nobles, Arthur M. Kassel, Antonio Gellini and Beverly Hills Mayor Thomas S. Levyn

(l-r) Helen Harris, Arthur M. Kassel, Antonio Gellini, Dianne Ladd and Phyllis Lycet at "Best of the Fests" at Universal Studios

(l-r) Antonio Gellini, Arthur M. Kassel and Dick Clark are pictured following the press conference at the Beverly Hilton

Landau at special screening

CBS Vice President of Specials Terry Botwick with actors Richard Thomas, Charlton Heston and Thomas Ian Nicholas announcing the Family Film Award nominees at the Beverly Hilton

Photography by Don Camp

ANTONIO GELLINI
Portrait of a Hollywood Legend

(l-r) Dr. Maria Simms, Howard W. Koch, Tichi Wilkerson Kassel and Antonio Gellini presenting a scholarship check to Gil Cates, Dean of the UCLA School of Cinema, at Mr. Koch's Paramount Studios office

Tichi Wilkerson Kassel
The former owner, publisher, and editor-in-chief of *The Hollywood Reporter*, Tichi is widely recognized as one of the most accomplished women in the history of show business. Her years of dedication to the industry were prominently noted when she was awarded her own star on the legendary Hollywood Walk of Fame. Tichi is the Founder and former President of Women in Film, which she established in 1972 to unite professional women in the industry. She also founded the *Hollywood Reporter* Industries Foundation (later renamed the Wilkerson Foundation) to provide grants and scholarships to foster journalistic and filmmaking potential in young people. Under Tichi's direction, the Wilkerson Foundation assisted in the creation and endowment of the Hollywood Women's Press Club scholarship program. She is also the creator of several industry awards, including the "Key Art Awards" and the "Marketing Concepts Awards."

Dr. Maria Simms
After having been among the youngest women to enter medical school in Argentina, Dr. Simms came to the United States and continued her education at Brigham Young University where she majored in Humanities. She went on to receive a degree from the University of California as a Medical Diplomat. Turning her attention to business, Dr. Simms is currently President of "Mid-Town Services, Inc." in Los Angeles, and "Lake Side Estates, Inc." in Arizona. She has been recognized in *Who's Who in the World* and *Who's Who in American Women*. Her many civic activities have included being Chairman of the Board of Directors of "Neighborhood for Peace, Inc.," an organization created to educate and help gang members get off the streets. She is also a member of such select organizations as "Southern California Alliance for Survival" and "Order for the Eastern Star."

Dr. Antonio Gellini at the Moscow International Film Festival, 1995.

MAKING HISTORY:
Moscow Film Festival

In 1995, against the advice of family and friends, Dr. Antonio Gellini traveled with several of his guests to the first Moscow International Film Festival, joining many other dignitaries and a number of actors and directors to open the film festival for the first time after the revolution. Among his entourage were various team members from World Film Institute as well as Bruce Malmuth (Director, Night Hawks starring Sylvester Stallone / Actor, The Karate Kid), Richard Gere, James Broling, Franco Nero and others. Included here are some still frame photos from the historic video footage that was preserved and will be released in the very near future.

The following appears in *Javanan Magazine* - Southern California Motion Picture Counsel. *(Author Unidentified.)*
https://www.facebook.com/javanan

This story has never been told. In May 1994, Antonio Gellini met Jack Valenti, the President and CEO of the Motion Picture Association of America, at the Cannes Film Festival.

ETHEL C. RICHARD
with Dr. Antonio Gellini

During the 50th Anniversary, every director of every festival from around the world came to celebrate with the dignitaries from every country. More than 3000 journalists witnessed the arguments of the various directors with their President, Jack Valenti. The argument was: why are Hollywood movies dominating the festival?

The last day of the festival, Antonio met Jack Valenti with the idea of doing a World Film Awards. This would be part of the 7 Arts of the Olympia Awards. Jack was so impressed by the idea that he invited Antonio to meet 56 directors of film festivals from around the world along with 3000 reporters. Jack said he never had the idea that Antonio had. This is the Ultimate Film Award, he said: choosing the best directors, stars, writers and actors from every category from ALL the festivals. This is the Best of the Best of everyone in the world. This will end all the arguments and appeal to the media and all the directors of every film festival around the world.

Later, Mr. Valenti introduced Antonio to Dick Clark, who immediately understood Antonio's goal and introduced him to his associate, Gene Weed, Country Music Awards Founder and Golden Globe Award Producer and Director. Mr. Weed began work with Antonio. Together, they signed with Ted Turner at CNN and TNT. At the Venice Film Festival, they announced the new Awards on Nov. 21st, 1995. And, for the first time, Antonio was invited by Ted Turner, Jane Fonda, Steven Spielberg, George Lucas and Sophia Loren to join the Academy of Motion Pictures Arts and Sciences

That night there was confusion that the World Film Awards

ANTONIO GELLINI
Portrait of a Hollywood Legend

would interfere with the Oscars.

Because of it, the studios joined together and gave 700 million dollars to Ted Turner to give up

CNN and TNT and to become Chairman of Time-Warner.

Photo of Jack Valenti

Antonio had a contract with Ted Turner and Dick Clark. He had the option to sue but chose not to. Then, Antonio saw the headlines of the LA Times, where President Clinton was critical of all the violence in movies and media. Antonio then called Jack Valenti about this with still another idea: every studio and network must make 3 movies a year that are family oriented. At the Century Plaza Hotel, Mr. Valenti and Dick Clark began a fund-raiser to initiate Mr. Gellini's idea. They introduced him to President Clinton, who totally supported

ETHEL C. RICHARD
with Dr. Antonio Gellini

Antonio's idea and put it into effect.

Now, Antonio came up with still another idea: a competition between all the family-oriented movies. He called it, the Family Film Awards. On August 22, 1996, CBS introduced LIVE from LA and NY, «THE FAMILY FILM AWARDS» with Bob Hope, Sandra Bullock, Ron Howard, Tom Hanks and a star-studded cast.

ANTONIO GELLINI
Portrait of a Hollywood Legend

ETHEL C. RICHARD
with Dr. Antonio Gellini

The Special was a huge success. Because of it Antonio received a five-year contract and a five-year option with CBS. But in 1997, Dick Clark had a debilitating stroke. Every major star from Eddie Murphy, Robin Williams and Billy Crystal offered to replace Dick Clark...but Antonio said he needed a year to think about it.

"God sometimes challenges us in ways we don't yet understand!" he said.

In 2012, Dick Clark died. Again, Antonio waited one year, out of respect to his culture. Confused, Antonio had no idea of how to replace Dick Clark and continue his mission. Then, one miracle day in April 24th, 2012, Antonio met his soul-brother, Allan Jay Friedman, Award Winning Producer-Writer and Composer, with a background in Law, Business and Public Health, who had created over 30 family-oriented movies, musicals and product lines. Impressed by Allan's 40 years of creative work, Antonio made Allan partner and President and CEO of the Family Film Awards.

After 29 years, Antonio then received a call to receive a major award at the United Nations for still another award he had created: the Olympia Award, the Olympiad of the 7 Arts of the World (music, art, literature, dance, sculpting, film and theater). Mr. Gellini then invited Mr. Friedman to be his Partner, President and CEO of the Olympia Awards as well and requested that he give a speech introducing his and Mr. Friedman's combined 80 years of work, which he and Mr. Friedman call, the «Dream of Camelot. » This historic event, in which Mr. Friedman spoke, will encapsulate both Antonio's and Allan's dream for the world: to transform it from being mind-driven to being heart-

ANTONIO GELLINI
Portrait of a Hollywood Legend

driven and to make it a free, safe and noble place for children.

The question I find most interesting is, what keeps this unusual man, Antonio Gellini, "going" through all of these mishaps and twists and changes? What keeps him focused and where is his ultimate grounding, where in reality was his pivotal moment during life in which he found his mission and envisioned it most clearly, that even today which keeps him daily on that path to it's constantly connected realization?

I include here statements made by Justin Wallner (Vice President of World Film Institute, Family Film Awards and Olympia Awards Games of 12 Arts and Entertainment and Exclusive Personal Publicist of Dr. Antonio Gellini).

"This is the story of a man whose Vision and Mission of creating a better world have been his guiding light from childhood and whose Right Thinking, Right Speaking and Right Actions were aligned at a very young age, guiding his influence upon history to the present day and beyond, attracting to this cause other highly aligned leaders who share his Vision and Mission of helping the world to shine bright through the full expression of humanity to Unify the Cultures of the world through the Universal Language of Arts in the name of Peace, Love and Light for all generations to come."

The year was 1995. Driven by a passion for art and the desire to share with the world the cultural diversity of his native Iran and the wonderful cities he hails from, Tehran and Mashhad, a young Antonio Gellini continued traveling the world to discover the diversity of other cultures and to share the beauty

ETHEL C. RICHARD
with Dr. Antonio Gellini

of his own.

After running the show "Locusts" at Iran Theater in his early days he was ready to see the world. He then traveled to Russia to compete in the Tashkent International Film Festival and then on to Germany to compete in the Berlin Film Festival, which he won with the film "Berlin Wall" at the young age of 17. After Germany he traveled to France to discover its cultural magnificence including the excitement surrounding the Cannes Film Festival. After France he was off to its great and mighty ally of old, the United States of America, and to the powerful city of Hollywood, California, known around the world and shining bright as the pinnacle city of arts and entertainment—not the least of which is Film.

1995 was also the year of the first World Film Awards—a competition which brought together the greatest films from cultures around the world, awarding one Winner from each of the Film Festivals of 56 countries who would then be entered into the final competition resulting in the awarding of one final World Film Awards Winner—the greatest independent film in the world.

Dr. Antonio Gellini and Mr. Dick Clark had a deal with Mr. Ted Turner, the Founder of Time Warner, to air the World Film Awards show on TNT on November 21st, 1995. It was to be the first time in history such a feat had been accomplished. Fearing they wouldn't be able to compete with this truly historic event involving independent films from the many nations of the world, various film executives gathered together from the Academy Awards and other organizations and filed a lawsuit

ANTONIO GELLINI
Portrait of a Hollywood Legend

against Dr. Gellini in a desperate attempt to stop him in court. That attempt was unsuccessful, however Mr. Ted Turner decided not to honor his contract and walked away from the $700 Million deal, of which Dr. Gellini stood to be paid $100 Million. Everyone was shocked.

Even more shocking is the fact that Dr. Gellini had an "open and shut" case against Mr. Turner, which he surely would have won had he taken legal action to claim his payment guaranteed by the contract—and chose not to pursue it. All he had to do for $100 Million was sign the claim but he refused. That shocked the world at the time and no one could understand why he took no legal action. When questioned, his answer was simple: "After all that America has done for me, I refuse to sue an American citizen."

1995 was also the year they broke the Disney monopoly on Family Films—an effort led by Dr. Gellini and his friends Mr. Dick Clark, Mr. Jack Valenti, then President of the Motion Picture Association and Mr. Bill Clinton, then President of the United States of America. A law was created requiring every Motion Picture Studio and all TV Networks in America to create no less than three (3) Family Films every year rated 'G' or 'PG' in order to stay in business. As a result, thousands of Family Films have been created in the last 21 years from all the major studios and all TV Networks in America, not just Disney.

This is a story that has never been told.

21 years later the epic saga continues to unfold once again—it started on August 27, 2015, when the Official Nominees of the 2nd Family Film Awards were announced at a most historic Press

ETHEL C. RICHARD
with Dr. Antonio Gellini

*Conference at the Universal Hilton Hotel in Universal City, CA. The final Winners of the long-awaited 20th Anniversary Family Film Awards of 2015 were announced at the 69th Annual Cannes Film Festival on closing day May 22nd, 2016. Winners were also chosen during the 70th **Anniversary** Cannes Film Festival for the 21st Anniversary Family Film Awards.*

In a statement made by Antonio Gellini from Cannes, France May 24, 2017: "I am embarking with the American Chinese Delegation on my fifth visit into China and while there I will tour eight provinces representing The Olympia Awards Competitions of Cultures, Arts and Entertainment before embarking on my trip into South Korea. You will see the Olympia Awards Competitions and the exchange of cultures which brings good into the world through these competitions ...and I am very proud to be a part of it.

MAKING HISTORY:
Family Film Awards

May 21, 2017 Former Vice President of the United States of America Al Gore catching up with his longtime friend Dr. Antonio Gellini, Founder and Chairman of World Film Institute presents Family Film Awards and Olympia Awards — at Marché du Film—Festival de Cannes.

Congratulations to all of our Family Film Awards Winners and Nominees this year and of years past! Former Vice President Al Gore On May 21, 2017 while announcing the Family Film Awards at our Breakfast Event during the 70th Annual Cannes Film Festival at Cannes, France stated his support for the 21st Anniversary Family Film Awards. Thank you to Al Gore for announcing the

ETHEL C. RICHARD
with Dr. Antonio Gellini

family film awards on May 21 at Breakfast,, and we thank you whole heartedly for your support! Also, thank you to InterContinental Carlton Cannes Hotel and management and Mr Andres Aguino (Couture Fashion Week) and especially to our producer for the 21 Anniversary Family film Awards, Mr. Alain Zirah and Miss Anne Gomis for the great reception of May 20 and thanks to the Director and Board of Directors for the 70 Cannes International Film festivals for their wonderful hospitality and great jury members and for announcing the winners of the Family film Awards 21st Anniversary on May 21 during the historic 70 Cannes International Film festival... I am very thankful to the great country of France. Congratulations to President Emmanuel Macron and First Lady Brigitte Macron and thanks to 70 Cannes international film festival and director of festival jury selection and all the french and international media for support in announcing the winners of the 2016 Family Film Awards on May 21st. God bless all and God Bless Family!

-Dr Antonio Gellini and
the Board of Directors for
the World Film Institute

OLYMPIA AWARDS OF CULTURES ARTS AND ENTERTAINMENT

2017 - 2018

21 years after Dr. Gellini refused to take legal action against Mr. Ted Turner, the Founder of Time Warner, planning is once again underway for the World Film Awards under a different name as it will be represented by the arts category of "Film" in yet another historic event—the Olympia Awards Games of the 12 Arts and Entertainment—honoring excellence in the 12 Arts of Dancing, Music, Painting, Sculpture, Literature, Theater, Film, Fashion, Culinary Arts, Humanitarian, Women and Special Needs.

2,792 years ago was the beginning of the first Olympics for Sports in Athens, Greece. Now, for the second time in history, a new Torch of the Greek Olympiad will be lit, once again, as the inaugural Olympics for the Arts begins in the land of a distant and very powerful descendant of ancient Greece—the United States of America, as participating countries (dignitaries and business officials) are collaborating together with the Institute on this event, planned to take place in Los Angeles in November, 2018. The whole purpose of the Olympia Awards Games of 12 Arts and Entertainment is to unify the world with Arts and Entertainment—the

ETHEL C. RICHARD
with Dr. Antonio Gellini

Universal Language and to transform the world from being mind-driven to being heart-driven

Not one to leave a historic task undone, Dr. Gellini is creating the American International Film Festival, a similar concept to World Film Awards as it will allow Winners from different cultures and Film Festivals around the world to compete in order to decide one final Winner of the American International Film Festival and the World Film Award. Similarly, the Olympia Award in Film will be decided through a competition of filmmakers that are first awarded in each of their respective countries resulting in a Final Winner of the Olympia Award in Film from all entries worldwide.

"In these times of change where the creation of visual images throughout the world and the powerful mediums that cut across lines are so important, I believe that we as filmmakers have an important responsibility because what we do affects the entire world. We can eliminate the boundaries of race, age, gender and religion through images that tell stories, represent adventure or impart information. From Indiana to India, from Chile to China, film touches one and all. God Bless Us All and God Bless America."

Dr. Antonio Gellini, Founder & Chairman of World Film Institute, the Family Film Awards and Olympia Awards Games of Culture, Arts and Entertainment Current members of the Board of Directors of World Film Institute, Family Film Awards and Olympia Awards Games of Culture, Arts and Entertainment are Dr. Antonio Gellini as Founder and Chairman, his business partner Mr. Allan Jay

ANTONIO GELLINI
Portrait of a Hollywood Legend

Friedman as President, Senior Vice Presidents Mr. Joel Diamond and Ms. Rossana Huang, Executive Vice President Mr. Ashkan Tabibnia, Vice President Mr. Justin Wallner who is also the exclusive personal publicist of Dr. Gellini. Mr. Kenneth Holm is the Chief Financial Officer and Mr. Koji Mizukami is the Secretary. The Advisory Board includes Mr. Mehdi Zokaei as President, Dr. Maria Simms as Vice President and Michelle Simms as a Board Member as well. Soon we will appoint more people from different studios and networks to various positions on both the Board of Directors and Advisory Board.

For more information please contact Mr. Justin Wallner at: **JustinWallner@GetGAMEPR.com**

And visit them online at:

http://www.antoniogelliniaworldforarts.care/

September 9, 2017 at Shanghai, China
Chairman of EU China Municipal Development Commission (ECMDC)
Mr. Zhang Yi, named New Chairman of World Film Institute Board of Trustees

The Chinese sign agreement with Antonio and this man, Mr. Zhang Yi (pictured above-left) becomes the Chairman of the Chinese, European Union, United States Board of Trustees for the World Film Association (a branch of The World Film Institute), which Antonio also founded and is the President and CEO. There are many photos from this event, far too many to show you here. However, as important as this event was, I found it pertinent to add a few here to wrap up this book.

ETHEL C. RICHARD
with Dr. Antonio Gellini

*Dr. Gellini and Mr. Zhang Yi outside
Beijing Office of World Film Institute*

ANTONIO GELLINI
Portrait of a Hollywood Legend

WORLD FILM INSTITUTE
Opening Ceremony and Welcome Tour in China

Details below of the royally extravagant Opening Ceremony and Royal welcome that Mr. Zhang Yi arranged to commemorate our new partnership and to celebrate the breaking of ground for our new World Film Institute office in Beijing, China from which we are laying the foundation for expansion in this great and beautiful country. We are helping to enrich the Chinese culture by showcasing the talent of her great artists in the film industry and beyond as we open the doors of cultural exchange and cooperation in film and arts between our great countries, reigniting the bonds between America and China which we hope will also enrich not only America and China but Hollywood as well, bringing Light to this city and to the world through various projects including the Chinese Family Film Awards, Olympia Awards etc.

The World Film Institute (WFI) is a non-profit organization focused on the advancement and recognition of multi-national film making and entertainment. The institute was founded by producer/director Antonio Gellini alongside interested filmmakers, production and distribution companies, and executives from the worlds entertainment centers. In today's fast changing world, the World Film Institute is a central organization that fulfills the desires for all

ETHEL C. RICHARD
with Dr. Antonio Gellini

cultures, races and nationalities to participate in the entertainment industry. Reaching beyond the "first world", the institute will strive to bring the possibility of film production to those who do not have access to equipment, training, distribution and recognition. The members of the World Film Institute receive advanced technical support services, training, scholarship, and information resources in an effort to meet film making needs globally. The recognition for excellent film making comes in the form of the Family Film Awards and the Olympia Awards. On August 21st, 2017, Mr. Zhang Yi and Mr. Antonio Gellini signed the Strategic Partnership Agreement between ECMDC and WFI in Beijing.

Mr. Zhang Yi will be the first Chinese who becomes Chairman of WFI Board of Trustees. ECMDC is dedicated to people-to-people exchange between Europe and China, of which Sino-European film industry cooperation is one of major components. ECMDC has established the close partnership with official film institutes of EU Member States, European film industry partners and European film schools. In the meanwhile, ECMDC has been engaged in the extensive and in-depth cooperation with Chinese film industry partners. Therefore, the new post as Chairman of WFI Board of Trustees will enable Mr. ZHANG Yi to integrate high-quality film industry resources of China, U.S. and Europe into one entity in order to guarantee the successful implementation of the concerned cooperation projects. ECMDC and WFI will work out the best road map for the joint efforts. Both parties will cling to the actual

ANTONIO GELLINI
Portrait of a Hollywood Legend

demands of people-to-people exchange within the framework of the Belt and Road, and aim to construct the world film cooperation platform by virtue of the tangible projects including the exchange of film products, the joint talent training of film industry and the exploitation of the international film market etc. ECMDC and WFI will jointly introduce the Family Film Awards and the Olympia Awards into China, and provide more and more windows for Chinese film industry professionals to participate in the exchange and cooperation with the international colleagues.

Mr. Antonio Gellini, Chairman of WFI and Mr. Justin Wallner, Vice Chairman of WFI visited China in recent days, and held the ceremony to officially appoint Mr. ZHANG Yi as Chairman of WFI Board of Trustees.

MESSAGE FROM THE FOUNDER

In these changing times, where the creation of visual images throughout the world can be shared through powerful mediums that cut across all boundaries, I believe that we as filmmakers have an important responsibility because what we do can affect the entire world. We can eliminate the barriers of race, age, gender and religion through visual stories that take viewers on an adventure or impart information. From India to Chile to China and even Hollywood, film touches one and all. I congratulate all who create art and images. I especially congratulate the Family Film Award and Olympia Award nominees in the past, and all those who will be nominated in the future. Your influence on the world is amazing and has the incredible power for change. I thank all those who have worked on the Family Film Awards in the past. The World Film Institute thanks DirectTV, Microsoft, PrimeStar and others for their sponsorship. I thank Dick Clark Productions for their vision that gave us a beginning in 1996. And I thank all those who currently have faced and met the challenge of taking the World Film Institute into the future.

With all our love and hope, we face the opportunity to create and bring change in the world. The World Film Institute and myself are committed to this change and all the possibilities it brings.

www.ingramcontent.com/pod-product-compliance
Lightning Source LLC
Chambersburg PA
CBHW040416100526
44588CB00022B/2840